Presented to Curt Sattazahn from
the Zion E. C. Church.

New Life,
New Lifestyle

New Life,
New Lifestyle

a fresh look at the world

Michael Green

MULTNOMAH PRESS
PORTLAND, OREGON 97266

I am grateful to the Rt. Rev. Hugh Montefiore for permission to quote his version of the Ten Commandments, and the Rt. Rev. Trevor Huddleston for permission to quote from a BBC broadcast. "Tonight will be Fine" by Leonard Cohen and "The Act of Love" by Roger McGough are reprinted from LOVE, LOVE, LOVE, edited by Peter Roche, published by Corgi Books Ltd. "Dial-a-prayer" is reprinted from Listen to the Green, © Luci Shaw, Harold Shaw Publishers, Wheaton, Ill. 60187. Used by permission.

Scripture quotations are from several versions, including:

The Holy Bible: New International Version, © 1978 by the New York International Bible Society. Used by permission of Zondervan Bible Publishers.

The Living Bible, © 1971 by Tyndale House Publishers, Wheaton, Illinois. Used by permission.

The New English Bible, © 1970 by the Delegates of the Oxford University Press and the Syndics of the Cambridge University Press.

Cover design by Mike and Doreen Button

NEW LIFE, NEW LIFESTYLE
© 1973 by Michael Green
Published by Multnomah Press
Portland, Oregon 97266

Printed in the United States of America

Library of Congress Cataloging in Publication Data

Green, Michael, 1930–
  New life, new lifestyle.

    1. Christian life—Anglican authors.   2. Conversion.
I. Title.
BV4501.2.G7452   1984   248.4'83   84-25390
ISBN 0-88070-073-4

84 85 86 87 88 89 90 – 10 9 8 7 6 5 4 3 2 1

For My Godchildren

Philip, Michael, Anne, Mark,
John and Paul

FOREWORD

One of the clearest truths of the New Testament—and yet one of the most easily overlooked—is that becoming a Christian is not only the end of an old life, but the beginning of a new way of life as well. The call of Jesus Christ is clear: "If anyone would come after me, he must deny himself and take up his cross daily and follow me" (Luke 9:23). Christ's call is not only to trust Him as Savior, but to follow Him as Lord. It is a life of obedience and discipline—but it is also a life of joy and peace.

This book sees all this plainly. My friend Michael Green has been greatly used of God to bring people to Jesus Christ, both through his unique ministry to St. Aldate's Church in Oxford, England, and through his worldwide lectures and preaching. More than that, however, God has wonderfully used him to help countless new believers understand what it means to be part of God's family and to grow each day in their relationship to their Lord.

In this book Dr. Green deals simply and clearly—and yet profoundly—with the practical problems and temptations that face the new believer. Drawing upon both his deep knowledge of the Scriptures and his wide experience in dealing with new believers, Michael points to the vast resources God has given us in His Word. I know of no book which deals so thoroughly and yet so readably with the essentials of the Christian life. Nor is Dr. Green content to speak in generalities. He tackles some of the hard issues of everyday life, showing that Jesus Christ can make a radical difference in the way we live and work and play . . . if we will but let Him.

It is right to think of this book as a primer for new Christians, and it certainly is that. But it is also a useful handbook which bears repeated reading. It

FOREWORD

cannot help but challenge and refresh Christians who have walked with Christ for many years.

Billy Graham

PREFACE

I am not one of those who believe that the Christian faith is on the way out. In many parts of the world, from South America to Indonesia, from Korea to Egypt, it is growing apace. In Britain and the States, too, there is widespread turning to Christ in situations where the church is not afraid to come out of its ghetto and proclaim the trenchant message of the New Testament gospel. In particular, there is a notable quickening of interest among students. Every year thousands of people leave atheism and other religions, hedonism and apathy, for Christian discipleship. It happens in universities and in youth groups, in clubs and on the streets, through preaching and through personal conversation: men and women surrender their lives to Jesus Christ, and they join the fellowship of the Christian family.

But when this happens, what is there to put into their hands? What contemporary book is there to give them, that will help them grow into mature Christians? Back in the early 1970s there was certainly not very much lively and readable material on so vital a subject. The lack of it drove both David Watson and myself to try to fill the gap, and he wrote *Live a New Life* (IVP) at the same time as I wrote *New Life, New Lifestyle*—quite independently of each other! Even in the decade since then little else has emerged to help the thoughtful new believer, apart from John White's *The Fight* (IVP), so I have revised *New Life, New Lifestyle* at the publishers' request. It is neither profound nor shocking. It is not comprehensive or even adequate. It is not scholarly or hard to follow. It is a simple book in which I have tried to paint on a broad canvas the main features of the landscape that unfolds before the new believer. It is meant to help people to "grow in grace, and in the knowledge of our Lord and Savior Jesus Christ".

PREFACE

I am grateful for permission to quote the copyright material. I have also found it illuminating to quote, anonymously, from my correspondence, much of it from new Christians. I am grateful to Edward England, Pat Dearnley, and Roy Catchpole for their assistance. Bible quotations come from a variety of modern translations, and sometimes from my own translations of the original.

Michael Green

CHRISTMAS, 1972   ST. JOHN'S COLLEGE,
NOTTINGHAM
ENGLAND

CONTENTS

1
TWICE IS THE ONLY WAY TO LIVE!

I heard about him recently. He is an Eskimo, the son of one of the last families to preserve their ancestral way of life—hunting, dog teams, igloos and all that. A nominal Christian, as so many of the Eskimo are, he got roped in to act as interpreter at an evangelistic meeting. As he interpreted, he began to trust Jesus Christ for himself. Previously he had no idea of the joy, the purpose and the new range of possibilities this would open up. But he has gone ahead at a great pace, and now is training for ordination at the tiny theological college in the Arctic. He is determined to spend his life spreading the good news of Jesus among his own people.

Not long ago I met a young man in his twenties who had been addicted to drink and drugs. One night when he was stoned with liquor and high on L.S.D. he heard about Jesus, the real living Jesus who could take him and change him. He surrendered his life to Christ, and the change began to take place. I met him ten months after this new beginning. He was radiantly happy, self-possessed and integrated. I asked him how long he had been a Christian. He told me, "Ten months." I asked him if he had introduced any others to Christ in this time, and he laughed—so did the others who were standing around in the flat in Toronto where this conversation was taking place. "More than I can remember" was his memorable reply.

I think of an occasion when I was teaching in a theological college. One of our students came to tell me that the previous weekend he had been revisiting a country parish where a team from the college had recently conducted a mission. One of his many encouragements was to sit at the back of a room where about thirty villagers of different ages, backgrounds and outlooks were engaged in a Bible study—led by a man and his wife who had found faith in Christ during the mission a couple of months earlier. It reminded me, as he spoke, of an R.A.F. officer who had become a believer in Christ through reading a book I had written. He gave copies to five couples among his military friends, and then invited them to meet my wife and myself in his home one evening. He sat down, put us at our ease and then explained why he had invited everyone there. He had only been a believer a few weeks himself, and had certainly never heard anyone speak about Jesus Christ to a group of friends in a home. He told us that he would not have believed it if anyone had informed him two months ago that he would be sitting at a group like that discussing Jesus; if they had gone on to suggest that *he* might be organizing the group, he would have thought them mad! But he had found Jesus Christ in the meantime—the living Jesus who had begun to make a new man of him. So naturally he wanted to share the news with his friends. You can imagine how well that evening went. His friends had expected me to talk about Christ—after all, I was a parson, and was paid to do that sort of thing. But they hadn't expected anything so definite, so full of a sense of discovery, from *him*. He was like the man in Jesus' parable, who had been plowing a dull and dusty furrow in a field, and then suddenly struck a box; on examination it turned out to be full of treasure. That's what it is like, according to Jesus, when someone discovers the Kingdom of God. It's like finding treasure, when you weren't expecting anything of the sort. Well, my friend had found treasure; and it made a great impression on his circle of friends.

All these people I have mentioned (and the list could be extended indefinitely) have one thing in common. They have found a new world of experience, a new dimension to living. It's as if they have been living in a pond all their lives up till now, like the tadpole. And now they have turned into frogs, and have emerged from the pond to start a fresh existence on dry land. Of course, like the frog, they are thoroughly at home in the pool still; they retain all the experiences they had before. But they have this new world opening up to them. It is almost as if they had been born all over again: that was, in fact, how Jesus described it to a learned theologian, who knew all about God and the Scriptures, but had never found the treasure of this new life.

New life

I am writing this book for people who have begun to emerge from the pool; for those who are making their first cries as babes in the family of God; for those whose eyes have been opened to a new world round about them, after Jesus has laid his hand upon them. I hope I am writing for you. I trust that you know what this new life in Christ means. If you do, you can skip the rest of this chapter. But if you don't, the next bit is rather crucial. Without it the rest of the book won't make any kind of sense. Lots of books on Christian behavior make the cardinal error of assuming you can lay down a code of conduct to be followed, and call it "Christian Ethics" *without changing human nature.* I tell you it can't be done. Incidentally, this is why we all feel that talk about morality is so dull and unattractive. It sets before us a standard which we can't keep; and that is depressing. It presents us with a set of rules; and that makes our hackles rise. We say, "Why should I bother with that one? Why should I keep this?" I have only to see a notice "Keep off the grass" and I immediately want to trample all over it. Don't you? Very well, we understand each other, you and I. We know that dead orthodoxy, codes of rules, moral behavior patterns leave us cold. To commend Christian ethics to people who have no Christian faith is simply asking for failure if they try to keep the standards, and for hypocrisy if they don't. It is as ludicrous as going around tying apples to a dead apple tree. The only way you will get any satisfaction with apples is to pick them off a live tree. You need to have Christ's new life coursing through your personality before you can produce the fruit of a Christlike character. Obvious enough, when you come to think of it. You can't have the new lifestyle without the new life.

Dead and alive

Fair enough. But how do you get the new life? The answer is not difficult. But it is costly. Costly to God, and costly to us. It is like this. God made mankind as the crown of creation. We share in and transcend the different levels of life displayed in the rest of creation. A stone has life of a sort; it exists. A flower has a more developed life, with its ability to breathe and to feed, to bud, to blossom and to die away . . . before the cycle begins again. Animals have a higher form of life, equipped as they are in varying degrees with mobility, intelligence, adaptability and strength. Some of the monkey family are almost human in their abilities. But there are very distinct differences between us and the animals. We can think. We can pray. We can communicate logically. We can make ourselves the object of our own reflection. We have a sense of beauty, of truth, of goodness. We have a conscience. In all these ways, and others, we transcend the animal creation. Our life is fuller than theirs. We rejoice in our physical, mental and aesthetic vitality. Especially if all of these are in good health, it is just wonderful to be alive.

But the Bible teaches, and experience confirms, that in a very real sense we are dead while we live. Dr. Herbert Kohn once wrote in a Sunday newspaper, "The biggest single problem facing us is no meaning and purpose. Why do we stay alive? What are we here for? My grandfather walked with God, and knew why—but we don't." That puts the human situation in a nutshell. In the graphic picture given us in the Book of Genesis, man was made to enjoy God's company—no less. We were meant to "walk with Him in the garden in the cool of the day." We were meant to enjoy this supreme dimension of life—sharing the very company of God who gave us life. Now the accent is on sharing. But what did man do? He decided to go it alone. He ate the fruit of the one tree that had been forbidden him. And disobedience broke the relationship. He ceased to walk with God. God was no longer a companion to be enjoyed, but a sinister figure to be dreaded. He might inquire, "Why are you hiding?" Feeling guilty, man preferred to keep out of God's way. Reluctantly God endorsed man's choice. He was expelled from the garden. He was cut off from what is picturesquely and significantly described as the Tree of Life.[1]

It makes little difference whether you take that story literally—and there's no compelling reason not to—or whether you regard it as a timelessly acute description of Everyman, a sort of Aesop's Fable, whose truth is not dependent on its mere historicity. On any showing, that is the human situation: We are aliens from our home. Indeed, so alienated are we, that it has been well said, "Modern man is no longer merely an exile. He has forgotten his home and has no hope of a promised land." We have rejected this highest range of life, sharing in the fellowship of our Creator, and spiritually speaking we are already dead. So dead that we are for the most part quite unaware of God's existence. So dead that we will not listen to his claims upon our lives. So dead that any talk about God seems utterly foreign to us, almost as if it were spoken in another language. Jean-Paul Sarte went so far as to claim, "God is dead, even in the hearts of believers." Indeed, many sensitive folk feel themselves to be "dead." Fellini, the film producer, and director of *La Dolce Vita*, wrote, "Like many people I have no religion and I am just sitting in a small boat, drifting with the tide. I just go on working, shooting, cutting, editing, looking at life and trying to make others see. Today we stand naked, defenseless and more alone than at any time in history. We are waiting for something— perhaps another miracle, perhaps the Martians—who knows?"

What Fellini was waiting for is a deliverer from aimlessness and death. But the man of tomorrow came yesterday. Jesus was his name. That word "Jesus" means, quite literally, "God to the rescue." Christians believe that Jesus was—and is—just that. I don't propose to argue the case for that stupendous claim. I have had to go at it in *World on the Run* and *You Must be Joking.* But I believe it with all my heart. I have scrutinized the evidence, and I am satisfied. So confident that I am prepared to gamble my life and destiny on its truth. And I believe that the whole objective in God becoming one of us for thirty years or so in the first century was to enable us to recover this "high octane" life, this possibility of life shared with him, which was lost by human disobedience in the mists of long ago, and which men continue to jettison daily as carelessly as they throw away a plastic cup.

Life through death

How was the situation of broken relationships to be restored, so that once again we could enjoy his life? Well, the essence of the operation was this. Jesus came, not primarily to teach men how to live, nor to heal the sick, nor to be an anti-establishment leader, but to bring new life to the spiritually dead. "I have come that they may have life, and have it to the full,"[2] said Jesus. St. Paul, reflecting on Christ's achievement, has this to say, "Time was when you were dead in your sins. In our natural condition we, along with all the rest, lay under the dreadful judgment of God. But God, rich in mercy, for the great love he bore us, brought us to life with Christ, even when we were dead in our sins."[3] The whole New Testament bears witness to the fact that it was through the cross and resurrection of Jesus that this new life has become available. We *can* live twice!

It is very difficult to understand how Jesus' death so long ago can be of any use to us today, and how it can make any difference to our relationship with God. There are various pictures sketched by the New Testament writers to help us understand. Sometimes they talk as if we were all captives in a foreign land to a hostile power, and the death of Jesus was the price paid to repatriate us and deliver us from this enemy power. But pursue that analogy too far and you get into trouble. You start asking to whom was the ransom paid, and at once you are in difficulties. So the wise thing to do is to look at another word picture and regain perspective. Sometimes St. Paul speaks of Jesus dying on the cross as the means of reconciling two estranged parties, us and God. Sometimes he speaks of Jesus as the mediator in a broken relationship (we have plenty of this sort of thing in industrial relations), and he only succeeded in restoring good relations at the cost of his own life. Sometimes New Testament writers see his innocent suffering as the ultimate way in which evil is conquered; once you retaliate you only double the evil. Jesus not only taught but demonstrated the tremendous moral power of the innocent willingly and lovingly accepting cruelty and brutality at the hands of the guilty in order to absorb and neutralize the wickedness and bring men to their senses.

All of these insights given us by the Bible writers shed some light upon his death. But perhaps the simplest and at the same time the most profound way of looking at it is this. *Our life was forfeit: he forfeited his life for us.* Perhaps that needs spelling out a bit. Our rebellion against God has cut us off from enjoying his company; we were "aliens . . . without God in the world."[4] Jesus, on the other hand, himself both God and man, himself tempted more strongly than any of us, nevertheless lived a life of perfect obedience. There was no rebellion against God in that life: rather, he could say with integrity, "I always do what pleases him."[5] He had no need to die, physically or spiritually. But die he did, by his own free and deliberate choice. He died physically in great agony on the cross, and spiritually in greater agony as he willingly made himself responsible for all the horrors, all the filth and guilt of man's rebellion, including yours and mine. He took your death, so that you could have his life. He died in the place the rebel should have ended up, so that the rebel could be adopted into the family from which he had played truant. He died that we might live—forgiven, accepted, in touch with God. Listen to the thrill of it coming over in Paul's writings. He never got over the wonder of it. "The Son of God . . . loved me and gave himself for me."[6] Or again, "Christ has bought us out from under the doom of that impossible system (i.e. trying to get back to God by working our passage) by taking the curse for our wrongdoing upon himself."[7] Or again, "We beg you, as though Christ himself were here pleading with you, receive the love he offers you—be reconciled to God. For God took the sinless Christ and poured into him our sins. Then, in exchange, he poured God's goodness into us!"[8] That idea of the exchange, his life willingly given for our lives that were forfeit, gripped the early Christians and made them deeply indebted to the love of the Lord. I think it explains why they gave so much notice to Barabbas in the story of the crucifixion. The cross on which Jesus died was meant for Barabbas. He deserved it, if anyone did. He was a robber, an insurgent and a murderer. Yes, he deserved to die. His life was justly forfeit. But Jesus took his place. He died on Barabbas' cross, though he didn't deserve to. And Barabbas went free because Jesus died on his cross, though he didn't deserve to, either. That exchange, so to speak, seemed to get to the heart of the meaning of the cross for the first disciples: Our life through his death.

Just after the New Testament period an unknown Christian wrote in these terms about what the cross meant to him: "He himself took on him the burden of our iniquities, the holy one for sinners, the immortal for mortals. For what else could cover our sins but his righteousness? O sweet exchange! O work of God beyond all searching out! that the wickedness of many should be hidden by a single righteous one, and that the righteousness of one should put many transgressors right with God."[9]

A few quick questions come to mind at this point. "Surely it is not fair of God to punish Christ for our misdeeds?" That is not what the New Testament says. It is not as though God was determined to take it out on somebody for the broken relationship, and if we were to get off scot-free, then he would make Christ pay. That is a travesty of the truth. No, we read, "God was reconciling the world to himself in Christ."[10] No third party was involved. God, in Christ, personally undertook to restore human relations with himself, though it involved nothing short of death and hell for him.

But again, people often ask me, "How can the death of Christ so long ago possibly be effective for sins that hadn't even been committed then—mine, for instance?" Part of the answer to this is to realize that the cross gives us a window into God's unchanging attitude towards human rebellion. He always has to judge it, and he always determines to taste its ashes himself so as to deliver us from the results of our wilfulness and folly (if we will allow him to). And part of the answer lies in the fact that Christ laid down his infinite life on that cross for the finite number of people in the world; and the finite, large though it be, is always outweighed by the infinite. On the cross we see God dealing in person, dealing at unspeakable cost, with the problem of human rebellion at its very root. Because he was going to do so, he could gladly accept anyone who lives A.D. The cross lies at the midpoint of time, and can avail for all.

"But does that mean that this new life you talk of is free, and that I have nothing to pay?" people ask. That is precisely what it does mean. Suppose you are in debt to the tune of thousands of dollars and are absolutely broke; and suppose your creditor says, "Right, you can go free: the debt is cancelled, and here's $20,000 to start you off in a new life"—what can you do but take it in wonder and gratitude, and say a heartfelt "Thank-you"? To attempt to pay for it would be as impossible as it would be impertinent. That, said Jesus, is the position we must take up before God's offer of a new life. We are his debtors, and he declares our debts discharged. We were doomed to death under his laws, and he tells us, "Your doom is remitted: you are free to live a new life." You can't pay for something like that. You can only take a Royal Pardon *as* a pardon; take it and be profoundly grateful.

But we have still only been considering half of the story. If the cross means that Jesus forfeited his life for ours which lay forfeit, the resurrection means that his new life can surge into our dead spirits. This is just what the early Christians found. To their amazement they discovered that Jesus was not dead and gone. He rose from the grave that third day; the tomb was empty, the last enemy defeated. Jesus had contested death, man's greatest foe, and he had overcome. "It was impossible for death to keep its hold on him," they concluded.[11] The only person who had lived a life of perfect obedience, Jesus was the only person on whom death, the fruit of human rebellion against God, could maintain no grip. He rose, and he is alive today, thank God. When a man becomes a Christian, it simply means that he allows this risen

Christ to come into his spirit and take up residence. And the Christian life is no less than Christ's own life struggling to show itself from inside us.

It is as if we own a filthy cottage which has never been cleaned, and eventually we accept the offer of a wonderfully generous spring-cleaner who is willing to come and put it right. We welcome him in, and he begins to clean things up. Foolishly we often hinder him, and put furniture in his way; we stir up the dust and refuse to let him clear up certain very private muck heaps. But gradually, progressively, he cleans up the house. And his order, his beauty, can be seen through the windows.

Or it is as if our life was a garden—derelict, overgrown, and devoid of fruit trees. The day we become Christians, the Spirit of the risen Christ is planted in our garden. It has to contend with lots of weeds which always hinder, sometimes threatening to completely stifle its growth. The climate is often cold, and the neglect to which the plant is subjected something awful. But gradually, over the years, the tender sapling grows into a fruitful tree, and people come and refresh themselves with the lucious fruit, even though there are still plenty of nettles round its base. This is how the new life of Christ takes root in our personalities and makes itself known even though every one of us still has a long way to go. St. Paul can rightly say, "The fruit of the Spirit is love, joy, peace, patience, kindness, goodness, faithfulness, gentleness and self-control."[12] Those lovely, mature fruits of Christian living are only possible when Christian life has begun, when the Spirit of the risen Christ has been welcomed into your life. Remember, it's no good tying apples to a dead tree. You achieve nothing, and only make yourself look ridiculous. You have to live twice!

From death to life

The issue is now crystal clear. It comes to this. Have you got new life? Has the Holy Spirit been planted in your life? "If anyone does not have the

Spirit," said Paul, "he is no Christian."[13] He may have been born in a Christian country, and have gone to a Christian school at the instigation of fond Christian parents. He may have attended church regularly and be able to say the Apostle's Creed backwards! But if he has not made room for the Holy Spirit to come into his life, whatever else he is, he is not a Christian. It sounds hard, but it isn't really. You see, he's still spiritually dead. He hasn't got the life of Jesus who died for his forgiveness, and lives for his transformation—he hasn't got this new life in him yet. A plant can't bear fruit until it has been planted and taken root. A person can't grow and develop until he has been born. Obvious, isn't it? And yet so many people fail to see it when it comes to spiritual things. You can't live the Christian life until you have been born into the Christian family. You can't produce Christian character until the Holy Spirit of Christ has been planted in your life.

Has he? You know if this has happened or not. You and God. If you know you have not begun, I suggest that before you go any further in this book, you get this matter sorted out once and for all with God. It doesn't matter how you express yourself; it's your attitude of giving in to God that matters. If it helps, you could say something like this:

> "God, I begin to see why you have seemed so unreal to me. I have been alive physically and mentally, but spiritually dead all these years, cut off from your life. No wonder I was very doubtful at times whether you even existed. But I do thank you very much for coming to meet me in my confusion. Thank you for Jesus and his amazing love in being willing to go to that cross for me. I don't understand it all, but I believe he did it for me, and that because he died there, I can be forgiven and have the past wiped out. That is a wonderful welcome, God, and I don't deserve it. I can't

begin to earn it. So I won't try. I will simply come to you and say 'Thank you.' And I am putting the rest of my life at your disposal. I want to use it for you now. I want the life of the risen Christ to come in and possess me. I want him to shine out through me. God, you have shown me through the cross of Jesus that you accept me, just as I am. Well, here and now I accept you. You're going to have to look after me, Lord, because I know I can't make it on my own. But then, I don't have to, do I? For you have promised that you will come and share your very own life with me. Please come in, Lord, and do just that."

You know, that James Bond film was quite right, more right than its producers realized. "You only live twice" . . . and twice is the only way to live!

NOTES

1. Genesis 3:24
2. John 10:10 (NIV)
3. Ephesians 2:1, 3-5 (NEB)
4. Ephesians 2:12 (KJV)
5. John 8:29 (NIV)
6. Galatians 2:20 (NIV)
7. Galatians 3:13 (LB)
8. 2 Corinthians 5:20, 21 (LB)
9. Epistle to Diognetus, 9
10. 2 Corinthians 5:19 (NIV)
11. Acts 2:24 (NIV)
12. Galatians 5:22, 23 (NIV)
13. Romans 8:9 (NEB)

2
GETTING IT STRAIGHT

When a man puts his hand in the hand of Christ, a new life begins. To quote St. Paul again, "When someone becomes a Christian he becomes a brand new person inside. He is not the same any more. A new life has begun!"[1] Sometimes the new life bursts exuberantly on the scene. This, for instance, is how one person wrote to me only five days after surrendering her life to Christ. She was a mature person, a mother, a strong character and an experienced hostess. She was certainly not the emotional sort. Would you understand what I mean if I tell you she was a brigadier's widow? Well, this is what she wrote.

> I must write and tell you what a tremendous experience this has been for me. No words can explain it. If anyone had told me last week that I should feel like I do this week, I am afraid I would not have believed it. In the past I have not prayed very much, or gone to church very much, and still I seldom read the Bible. I want you to know that it was for this reason that I wavered so long on Saturday

> morning, taking so much of your time. I did not think I could be ready to take such a step. But how right you were, and my heart is full of thankfulness: to Graham for bringing me to you, to you for bringing me to Christ, and to Christ, above all, for entering in, for there is absolutely no doubt about it. In fact I still feel rather in the clouds, but I know that there is a lot of work to be done as soon as I return home. . . .

Yes, some people feel like that immediately when they start the new life. But some people don't. Here is another reaction after almost exactly the same period of a few days.

> Really, I scarcely know what has happened to me this week. Perhaps this is the best test of the validity that God really did respond and come into my heart—that there was no spectacular emotional experience, of which I would have been very mistrustful; but somehow there really was something different. I felt as if I was being pushed from one thing to another all through the usual routine, by something inside me. Instead of frantically trying to plan my time to fit everything in, I scarcely had to think about it. I'm still afraid that the assurance will not last. I didn't really believe that I could have a personal relationship like this with God, so I suppose it is natural for me to be surprised and rather unsure of it. It's too soon to say "It has made such and such a difference to my life." At present I just want to get to know him better.

That last sentence could almost be the theme of this book. It is the authentic Christian longing. Having found Christ, we want to explore him more and more, and to give ourselves over to him in every department of our lives. That is the very heart of the Christian life: getting to know him better, and working out the implications of it in our behavior and attitudes, our career and relationships.

We shall be examining some of these areas in subsequent chapters. But there is a prior issue to sort out. It came up in both of these quotations from my correspondents. It is the problem of what to do with our doubts, and how far we should allow our Christian assurance to be governed by our feelings.

Dealing with doubts

There are a good many uncertainties and doubts we cannot avoid; and in our own generation these are far more pressing than ever before. Insecurity arising from unemployment, hunger, political and industrial unrest, broken relationships; and hovering over it all, the threat of the nuclear bomb. These are uncertainties we have to live with. However, we can have, and are meant to have, complete confidence that we belong to Christ. Indeed, unless we are sure about this relationship with him, we shall neither be able to develop it nor to introduce others to him. We would be building the house of our lives on sand instead of rock.

But doesn't any suggestion that the Christian can be sure where he stands smack of smugness and self-confidence? That is an accusation often made, but it is simply not the case. Of course, there are Christians who are smug, but that is their fault, not the fault of their Christianity. It is possible to be sure without being smug.

Suppose you give your child a bicycle for Christmas. You mean him to know that, don't you? He can be sure of your gift, but he has nothing to crow about. He didn't earn it; it's a gift.

Now it is like that with God. If we start thinking about what we deserve, then the New Testament tells us straight: "The wages of sin is death." We do not and cannot earn new life. "The *gift* of God is eternal life in Christ Jesus our Lord."[2] New life is his gift. I know I've got it, but I also know it is entirely due to his generosity, not to my merits. That is what the famous phrase "justification by faith" means. We are justified, acquitted, put in the right with God (a status which nothing can destroy) not by our "works," our efforts at self-justification, but by "grace," God's undeserved favor to us.[3] And this we receive by "faith," by trusting him. "So now, since we have been justified by faith, we can have real peace with God because of what Jesus Christ our Lord has done for us. In response to our faith, he has brought us to this place of highest privilege in which we stand, and we rejoice in the expectation of becoming all that God has in mind for us to be."[4]

Is it wrong to be sure?

What I want to ask those Christians who believe it is wrong to be sure about relationship with Christ, is this. "Do you know what family you belong to? Do you know if you're married?" Of course they know, and would never dream of saying, "Well, I *think* I am in the Green family and that my name is Michael, but I'm really not sure," or, "I think I'm married; I hope I'm married; but it is presumptuous to say that I *am* married." What nonsense that would be. It is just as nonsensical and much more impertinent to doubt God. He says that we are the bride, and Christ is the bridegroom; we are linked to him forever in the closest of all possible ties. He says that he adopts us into his family, so that we are sons in the family of God, and fellow heirs with Christ of all his bounty.[5] He says it, he means it and we can take him at his word.

It comes down to this, really: Trust. As in all personal relationships, trust is fundamental. How does the wife know her husband won't cheat on her? How does the patient know the doctor won't poison him? How does the client know the lawyer won't swindle him? How does the child know that his mother loves him? The answer in each case is simply trust. Why should it be different with God?

Look: Christ says he will accept you. "Whoever comes to me I will never drive away."[6] And you have come to him, as best you know how? Very well then, he *has* accepted you, for the simple and utterly sufficient reason that he said he would. Your feelings may be up or down; it matters not one whit. Your experience is nil to start with. You have nothing but his naked word to go on. But it is enough. It brought assurance to Dr. Livingstone over a century ago as he struggled with doubt and loneliness in the jungles of Central Africa. He recorded in his journal his reflections on the promise of Jesus I have just quoted. And his comment was, "That is the word of a gentleman of the most strict and sacred honor. He cannot break his word." A very Victorian way of putting it, but the point is good enough.

I well remember a man calling me on the trans-Atlantic telephone. I had only met him once before, and then he was an alcoholic, estranged from his wife and family, and fighting hard against the love of God. One night, just before I left Canada, he handed over his life to Christ, and the next I heard of him. two months later, was this phone call. He asked if he could come to the theological college, of which I was principal, for two terms in order to get established in the Christian life. I had to make a lightning decision: I said, "Come." He replied, "Right, I'll be there tomorrow night."

Now what would he have felt like if some had asked him, "What, *you* accepted in St. John's, Nottingham? Have you got the academic qualifications? Have you supplied names of references? Have you any idea how you'll make out? Have you any money to pay?" His answer to all these points would have to have been "No." He had one thing, and one only, to rely on if he was in any doubt about his acceptance. He had my word. That was all. And he trusted it. That is precisely what you do with the promise of the God you can't see when he says you are accepted into his family

31

even though you have done nothing to earn your adoption certificate, have nothing to pay, have no idea of how it will all work out and cannot quote good references for yourself. You trust his word for a start. And, as a matter of fact, you have something more to hold on to in this respect than my Canadian friend had. You have baptism.

The mark of belonging

Baptism is the mark of Christian belonging. Christians in the Baptist tradition believe this should be by total immersion and only after you have put your faith in Christ. Many other Christian churches believe that it is immaterial whether baptism precedes faith or faith precedes baptism, so long as the Christian both believes in his heart and has this outward mark of baptism upon him. But both traditions are clear about its importance.

You have only to go to a predominantly Muslim or Buddhist country to discover how baptism sets someone apart. He may believe secretly, and nobody worries too much; but as soon as he gets baptized, then he has to face the music. I remember several of my Jewish friends of student days being disowned by their parents because they had confessed Christ not merely in personal faith but in open baptism. Baptism is, therefore, very much the mark of discipleship: the irrevocable pledge that I belong to Christ and am committed to being "his faithful soldier and servant until my life's end."

It is important to stress the decisiveness of Christian baptism, as the mark to others that I am a follower of Christ. It is even more important to stress the decisiveness of Christian baptism as the mark God gives to me to assure me that I belong. If, in a moment of doubt, a young bride separated from her husband finds herself wondering whether she is really married or whether it is all just a dream—she has only to glance down at her ring. There it is, the mark of belonging, the love gift from her bridegroom to assure her that she does belong to him for keeps. Baptism acts as a physical reassurance of our relationship to Christ. He accepts us, forgives us, adopts us into his family and offers us his Holy Spirit to live in us, not because we have done a thing to deserve it, but simply because God is love. In his love he came to this world for us. In his love he died for us. In his love he welcomes us, irrespective of our qualifications. And baptism graphically declares all this.

This is important: All Christians should be baptized. If you have committed your life to Christ and have not yet been baptized, you are clearly bidden by the New Testament to get baptized. Baptism and belief belong together as the visible and the invisible side of the same relationship.[7]

The point I want to stress is this. Your baptism is not only the mark of your faith, but of God's gracious acceptance of you. Seen in this light it is a visible, tangible promise. It is as if God says to you by it, "Yes, I know you have let me down, since you came to faith. I know you are racked with doubts. But I have given you this mark of baptism in your body to assure you that you are accepted, unacceptable as you may be in yourself. You are now in the family, through my dear son, Jesus Christ." It was Martin Luther, the man who set Europe ablaze with his teaching on justification by faith, who struck such a helpful note on this subject. In the times of depression and doubt which afflicted him he took courage, not by saying to himself, "I have believed." That would have put the spotlight on himself, and it was himself and his faith that he was doubting! No, he said "I have been baptized." It was the mark that God had adopted him, Martin Luther, unworthy though he was. It was the badge of belonging, the standing reminder that Christ had accepted him, just as he had accepted Christ.

As time goes on, you won't be tempted to doubt in the same way as you are tested initially. There's no point. The devil realizes it is a dead loss to tempt an old, experienced Christian with doubts about whether he has really begun the Christian life. I may have thought it incredible that Rosemary, my wife, should care about me in the earliest days of our love, but now we've been happily married for years and doubts of her love never cross my mind. We have had too much experience of living together to doubt its reality and the strength of our relationship. And it is like that with the Christian. As the months and years go by you will discover that the devil finds plenty of other ways of tripping you up, but leaves this initial gambit pretty much alone. You will also discover that you have become as sure of your relationship with Christ as you are with some friend you know and love well.

A Letter for doubters

One of the New Testament letters was written for people who had not so long ago entrusted their lives to Jesus Christ. St. John tells us at the end of his Gospel that its supreme purpose was to bring people to the conviction that Jesus was God's Son; and further, to that personal encounter with Jesus that would start them off on a new life. He wrote his first letter, he tells us, to people who already believe in Jesus, so that they may know that they have eternal life[8]—this new quality of existence of which we spoke in chapter one. Notice that word "know." We are meant to be in no doubt about it. And in that letter John outlines several of the ways in which the new life will make itself felt.

New sense of pardon

There's a new sense of forgiveness. The man who couldn't even forgive himself is assured, as he looks at the cross, that he is forgiven so far as God is concerned. "If you sin, there is someone to plead for you before the Father. His name is Jesus Christ, the one who is all that is good and who pleases God completely. He is the one who took God's wrath against our sins upon himself, and brought us into fellowship with God; and he is the forgiveness for our sins, and not only ours but all the world's."[9]

34

New desire to please God

Then there's a new desire to go God's way. Previously I did not care too much if I did wrong, so long as I was not found out. But now I do begin to care—even if nobody is watching. Because I know that wrongdoing was the thing that took my Lord to the cross. It hurts him. And I don't want to hurt the one I have begun to love. "Someone may say, 'I am a Christian; I am on my way to heaven; I belong to Christ.' But if he doesn't do what Christ tells him to, he is a liar . . . That is the way to know whether or not you are a Christian. Anyone who says he is a Christian should live as Christ did."[10]

New attitude to others

Here's a third pointer: A new attitude to other people. "This is how we know who the children of God are and who the children of the devil are: Anyone who does not do what is right is not a child of God; neither is anyone who does not love his brother."[11] In other words, we see the man next door not just as a nasty piece of work (which he may very well be—but then so are we until Jesus gets to work on us). We see him as the nasty piece of work for whom Christ was content to die. And if Jesus did that for him, well, it rather changes things does it not? We begin to see others as Christ sees them, and to act accordingly.

New care for Christians

There's a very special side to this new love which characterizes Christians. It is a love for other believers, a sense of belonging to them in the same family. Indeed, so significant is this that John gives it as one of the ways of deciding whether a man is a Christian or not. "If we love other Christians it proves that we have been delivered from hell and given eternal life . . . We know what real love is from Christ's example in dying for us. And so we also ought to lay down our lives for our Christian brothers."[12] That is just what the early Christians did, and it so impressed the world that men exclaimed, "See how these Christians love one another." Sadly, in many churches today there is little of that infectious gaiety and unselfish love for brother Christians; instead, you find rather a carping and critical spirit. But that is not the true family characteristic. I have had the chance in recent years of going into many parts of the world, Africa, the Far East, Australia and North America, and I have been more than ever struck by this love for fellow Christians which always springs from true conversion. You may never have seen the chap before; you may never see him again. But even in a short meeting you seem to go right down to bedrock with another member of the Jesus family. You feel that you have known him for years. You sense that you are on the same wavelength, both forgiven sinners, both men with a message and a new purpose in life, both with the same Holy Spirit at work changing you from inside. This love for brother Christians, irrespective of color, background or nationality,[13] is one of the most precious gifts God gives his children—and thereby assures them that they really do belong.

New power over evil

Do you want another sign of the new life surging within? Here it is. "The person who has been born into God's family does not make a practice of sinning, because now God's life is in him; so he can't keep on sinning, for this new life has been born into him and controls him—he has been *born again*."[14] In other words, there is a new power released within the Christian, none other than Christ himself who is now resident inside us. Of course, Christians can and do sin. John knows that perfectly well.[15] What is more, he knows the way of pardon for the guilty Christian conscience—as we come straight back to our heavenly Father, tell him the mess we made and rely on his forgiveness, which is guaranteed to us by the cross of Jesus. But sin should increasingly become the exception, not the rule. The new life in us does not do what is wrong, because it is God's life at work in us. In so far as we allow that new life free play, we shall find that the power of Christ does deliver us daily from the forces of evil that have for so long dragged us down. It was interesting that the first letter I had from my Canadian friend, whom I referred to previously, made this very point about a new power let loose in his life. "I purposely have not written to you until now, because I wanted to see if what had happened to me would last," he wrote after a couple of months. "It has lasted! . . . My craving for alcohol and cigarettes left me immediately, and I have had no desire for either of them since." How about that? The power of alcoholism, and the power of smoking were snapped overnight, as if the Lord was giving him a foretaste of what he could do. Of course he had a long way to go. There were plenty of battles to come, and he may have had a presentiment of them in writing what followed. "My resentments are gone, and my fears, but I find that when I'm not watching they can sometimes creep up on me again." Don't we all? What is the way to meet them, then? My friend had already discovered it. "So I have to keep on coming back to God. But the big difference is that now I have him to come back to." The Christian life begins with Christ and continues with Christ. He is the only one who can change us. And the wonder of it is that he does, if we let him, and just as much as we let him. It is perfectly true that "every child of God can obey him, defeating sin and evil pleasure by trusting Christ to help him."[16]

New joy and confidence

There are other things that gradually emerge as we press further and further into the new country of life with Christ. For one thing, there is the joy he gives. Why, St. John says that he wrote this letter "so that you, too, may be full of joy," a joy that comes from "our fellowship with the Father and his Son Jesus Christ."[17] For another thing, there is the still, gentle voice of the Holy Spirit inside us assuring us that we are in the family. "The man who believes in the Son has this voice of testimony within him," says John, "the voice of the Holy Spirit in our hearts."[18] It is not easy to describe what this means to anyone who has not experienced it, any more than it is to describe what it means to be loved to someone who has had a loveless life. John does have a go at it in another place in his letter. "We know how much God loves us because we have felt his love and because we believe him when he tells us that he loves us dearly. God is love, and anyone who lives in love is living with God and God is living in him. As we live with Christ, our love grows more perfect and complete; so that we will not be ashamed and embarrassed at the day of judgment, but can face him with confidence and joy, because he loves us and we love him too."[19] If you've been a Christian even for a short time, you'll understand what John is talking about. That is what is meant by the inner witness of the Holy Spirit.

New experience of prayer

One other thing begins to change: prayer. We shall have more to say about that in chapter four, but just for the moment notice this. John marvels at the new experience of answered prayer which opens up once we come into the family of God. In the old days, nobody seemed to be there; nobody seemed to listen. Prayer was a hopeless exercise; it did no good; and probably we gave it up entirely, except perhaps as a last resort in some emergency. Look at the change now. "This is the assurance we have in approaching God: that if we ask anything according to his will, he hears us. And if we know that he hears us—whatever we ask—we know that we have what we asked of him."[20] A new world, you see. No longer is God a stranger, but a friend, a father, one who delights to have us talk to him, and open up the whole of our lives to him. And, no less amazing, we begin to want to do it. We actually come to enjoy prayer. Fantastic, but true, as any Christian will tell you. It is one of the signs of new life.

So these are some of the marks of God's new vitality which gradually makes itself felt in different aspects of our life. They take time. But they do come. They justify Paul's tremendous claim with which we began that "when someone becomes a Christian he becomes a brand new person inside. He is not the same any more. A new life has begun!"[21] But they don't happen all at once. So to begin with, rely on the promises of Christ. Learn some of them by heart. Do you remember the story of Christian in Bunyan's *Pilgrim's Progress*? The newly converted Christian strayed off the King's High Way and got imprisoned by Giant Despair in Doubting Castle. He almost gave up hope of ever getting out, until he recalled that he had on him all the time a key which would fit the lock, the key "Promise." Hold fast to the promises of Christ when you are tempted to doubt. They are the sure way out from the dungeons of Doubting Castle.

Notes

1. 2 Corinthians 5:17 (LB)
2. Romans 6:23 (NIV)
3. Ephesians 2:8, 9; Romans 3:24, 25
4. Romans 5:1, 2
5. 2 Corinthians 11:2; Romans 8:15, 17
6. John 6:37 (NIV)
7. Romans 6:3, 4; Galatians 3:24-27
8. 1 John 5:13
9. 1 John 2:1, 2 (LB)
10. 1 John 2:4, 6 (LB)
11. 1 John 3:10 (NIV)
12. 1 John 3:14, 16 (LB)
13. Colossians 3:11, 12
14. 1 John 3:9 (LB)
15. 1 John 1:8, 9
16. 1 John 5:4 (LB)
17. 1 John 1:3, 4
18. 1 John 5:8, 10
19. 1 John 4:16-17 (LB)
20. 1 John 5:14, 15 (NIV)
21. 2 Corinthians 5:17 (LB)

3
A FRESH PERSPECTIVE

He was writing to me to describe the change in attitude that had come about since he became a Christian.

> It is rather like a cyclist who, when he has climbed a long hill, feels he should be able to free-wheel down the other side. It is not until he reaches the top that he sees that his task has only just started, and that the road winds on, with even steeper hills than the one he has just climbed. When people accept Christ, they tend to think it will all be free-wheeling from that point. But then they discover it is only the beginning. At least, that's the case in my experience.

And in mine too. Now why should this be?

It is important to get clear about this right away because it is bound to influence the way we approach the rest of our Christian life. Why is it harder once you have become a Christian than ever it was before?

Going with the crowd

It is harder because in the old days you were largely influenced by what *you* wanted to do, or by the group you went around with, or what happened to be the fashion of the moment. On the whole you saw no particular reason to be different, unless it suited you to be. You went with the crowd. It was more convenient that way. Anyhow, what could one individual do, even if he wanted to? So why bother? According to most people, right and wrong are just matters of personal choice or convention. They don't hold good for all men everywhere. So why not take the easy way, the way that pays best? After all, the world isn't going anywhere. There is nothing that ultimately matters. We came from nothing and we are going to nothing. So make the best of it. Get as wide a range of experience out of life as you can. That's what it's there for. If you should die young, it would be a pity to have missed any of it. So by all means smoke marijuana and sleep with whom you like, provided nobody gets too badly hurt. It will be interesting to find out what each new experience is like. And why not? There is no heaven or hell, neither God nor devil . . . or *is* there a devil after all? There's certainly something in all this Satan worship and black magic. But anyhow, there is no God. Of that we can be sure. So nothing is forbidden unless of course you personally don't like it. Do your own thing and enjoy it. I'll do mine.

Those are among the current attitudes of modern people, especially young people. And they are very reasonable, too. Reasonable in a way their parents' outlook on life was not. For Dad's generation did not believe in God any more, as his father's generation had done. Yet Dad still occasionally went to church so as to keep up appearances, and make a friendly gesture towards the God who was dead. Dad still thought it was wrong to commit adultery (even if he did it) and right to tell the truth (even if he didn't). In other words, members of Dad's generation were very often hypocrites, though they would hate to have been told it. They didn't believe in God, and yet they made some attempt to behave as though he was still around—at least in the background.

But now a generation has arisen that has no time for this sort of play-acting. Science has ditched God. We came from plankton and we go to extinction. This life is a short and ultimately meaningless interlude, a sick joke in a basically impersonal universe. Right, we'll draw the consequences from that position. It's no good wishing things were different, or hoping that we have a life after death. We haven't, and that's all there is to it. So you'd better make the most of this one; for that's your lot. "Is God dead?" asked Ivan Karamazov in Dostoyevsky's great novel: "then everything is permitted."

Let's have a look at this more closely. What I am saying is this. Modern man has knocked the Absolute out of his world, and he is left only with the relative. There is no absolute standard for human behavior left—so men can set up their own standards of what is acceptable. There is no absolute standard for truth left, and so even the philosophers have given up trying to discover truth, along with justice, goodness and the other great subjects they used to pursue; instead they have taken to analyzing words! You have only to watch a representative sample of modern films and plays to realize that they carry a message, a very clear message—that life is meaningless. Rationality is commonly subordinated to feeling. "Is it true?" gives place to "Is it relevant?" Much new legislation is no longer based on principle, but on attempting to determine what most people want. In industry, or in personal relationships, the notion of "I want" is paramount: "I ought" is at a discount. It is the terrible but logical outworking of atheism.

Swimming against the current

Now do you see why it is harder to be a Christian than it was to stay uncommitted? Then you swam with the current. Now you are up against it in every conceivable way. You have dared to put the Absolute back into the picture. You have recognized God as the center of all existence, and you have gotten in touch with him. You belong to a minority, a guerilla band. You are out on your own.

Others may think life has no meaning. You know it has. It is meant to be shared with the Source of all being.

Others may think that the world is the result of a fluke or the influence of the stars. You know it is the product of a wise and loving Creator.

Others may think that the universe is silent and unfeeling. You know it shouts aloud of your loving heavenly Father who made it, and who discloses himself in the color and scent of every rose or the glory of every sunset.

Others may think that human personality is a quirk of luck in a world that is basically mechanistic. You know that it is the highest gift of a personal God. That's why human beings matter so infinitely. They are made in his likeness.

Others may think that truth and beauty and goodness are merely a matter of taste. To you, they are different aspects of the Lord himself, who is the acme of goodness, the source of beauty and the essence of truth.

Others may see that love is the one hope for mankind, but have no answer to the problem of why we should bother to love and how we can manage to do it. For you, love is the personal trade mark of the Creator, himself Love, who has shared something of his very nature with us—even with those who don't believe in him. And as a Christian you bother because all men are the objects of that love of his; you cannot manage to love folk by your own efforts. It didn't take you long to discover that. But once allow the love of God to reach you and it's bound to find a way out through you to others.

Everything, yes everything, is different, once God is restored to his rightful place. And you have done that, have you not? He is in the middle of the picture? Then don't be surprised that things are tough. What revolutionary ever had them easy? And Chris-

tianity is for revolutionary spirits, not for pale confor-
mists. It is for people who have the guts to be different.

A changed life—God's will

I think the greatest area of difference is going to
be our behavior. And you will have noticed that this is
precisely what people expect. No sooner claim to be a
Christian at work than they will expect you not to
swear and not to tell dirty stories. They will expect you
to clock in on time and work hard. No matter what
they may say about not wanting Holy Joes about the
place, ordinary non-religious people expect a Christian to be different and to have higher standards than
themselves. And that, though it is rather embarras-
sing and challenging, is a healthy instinct. I'll tell you
why.

Wherever you look in the religions of the world,
you will find no essential link between religion and
morality, except in the religion of Israel which flow-
ered in Christianity. You worshipped a god or gods in
the pagan religions of the ancient world, so as to have
an insurance policy in times of trouble, and in order to
fulfill the instinct to worship which is found in every
nation under the sun. But your worship did not make
many—if any—ethical demands on you, apart, maybe,
from a few taboos, such as a ritual bath or abstinence
from sex relations for a few days before worship. Worship and morals were not linked.

But with Israel it was different. They didn't seek
after God. He sought after them. He revealed himself
to them from Abraham's day onwards, not only as the
one object of worship big enough for man, but as the
very source of man's instincts about right and wrong.
"Ethical monotheism" is what the pundits call it: one
God and one alone—the source of morals and the goal
of ethics. All through the Old Testament days you find
this emphasis. It was not a bit of good worshipping
the Lord if the worshipper then went out to "sell the
needy for a pair of shoes." God was not to be kept quiet
with a church service at the weekend while people

continued oppressing the poor and swindling their neighbors in the weektime. As long ago as the eighth century B.C. Amos was scolding the Israelites for driving a wedge between their religion and their conduct:

> He who made the starry universe,
> Who turns darkness into morning light
> And darkens the day into nightfall,
> Who summons the waters of the sea
> And pours them out on the face of the
> earth,
> This is the One whose name is the Lord.[1]

And the Lord was appalled by what he saw in Israel, his people, who ought to have understood. Religion in plenty, but no changed lives; no sign of being transformed by the holy God they claimed to worship. His reaction?

> I loathe and despise your festivals;
> Let me have no more of your noisy hymns;
> My ears are closed to the music of your
> harps.
> Instead let justice roll on like a mighty
> river,
> And integrity flow like a never failing
> stream.[2]

Far from loving justice, the leaders in the nation "hate the honest witness in court, and loathe men of integrity. They trample on the weak and compel him to give them loads of grain. They browbeat honest men, take bribes and ignore the poor man's claim for justice." Their womenfolk "glitter on the heights of Samaria, but defraud the poor and ride roughshod over the needy, while they keep ordering their husbands 'Bring us wine to drink.'"[3] For this reason God would not and could not relent. It was no longer credible that Israel represented him. The whole nation would have to go into exile. And it did.

The need for righteous living among those who claim to worship a righteous God could scarcely be more strongly emphasized. God, the source of all that is good and true and upright, demands these same qualities in his worshippers. Not, mind you, as a condition of accepting them. We have already seen that he accepts us just as we are. But in due course he does expect the family likeness to become visible in members of his family.

He has gone to considerable trouble to make himself plain on that point. He does not leave us with mere generalities, evocative though they may be, like, "Be holy, because I am holy," says the Lord.[4] Throughout the Bible, and particularly in the Old Testament prophets, God lets us know what this holiness of character is going to mean in ordinary, daily behavior. But we aren't very good, on the whole, at listening to other people, even if they are prophets, lecturing us about right and wrong! We are much more liable to be moved by a good example. So that is just what God, in his generosity, provided.

A changed life—Jesus' example

Jesus Christ came not only to be our rescuer from the mess we had got ourselves in, but to be our example of the right way to live. He lived the perfect life. Never a foot wrong. Never a word out of place. Never a loving act neglected. Never a need unmet. In Jesus Christ we see the ideal for human life. Perfection walked this earth in his person. We no longer need to wonder what the good life might involve. We can no longer plead ignorance. It is there before us, plain for all to see. Unlike any other teacher before or since, Jesus actually lived up to his own teaching. He who told men to love their enemies did that very thing. He who told men not to lay up treasure on earth was so poor that he had no home. He who told men not to worry about their food and clothes lived a life of radiant peace despite the lack of what we would consider even the necessities of life.

Examine the moral teaching of Jesus and I think you'll find that he completely lived up to his own standards. His life was a moral miracle. He showed us not just by his unique teaching but by his matchless living what holiness meant, what the character of God was like. And the implication was painfully obvious. "Christ is your example," cried Peter (and he should know, having lived three years in Jesus' company, watching his every move). *"Follow in his steps!* He never sinned, never told a lie, never answered back when insulted; when he suffered he did not threaten to get even; he left his case in the hands of God who always judges fairly."[5]

But does that really help? It is one thing to recognize that the God we worship is holy and expects us to get increasingly like him. It is another to realize that he has given us a personal demonstration in terms of a human life to show us what he means by practical holiness. But my trouble is, how can I begin to match up to a standard like that?

A changed life—the Spirit's power

Well, once again, God has made the necessary provision for us. Paul puts it in a nutshell in his first letter to the Christians in Thessalonica, fresh converts from paganism in northern Greece. In almost the same breath he sets before them Christian standards, "God wants you to be holy and pure," and Christian resources, "God gives us his Holy Spirit."[6] The holy God does not lower his standards. He gives us the Holy Spirit to enable us to keep them. God's Holy Spirit is none other than Jesus Christ in spirit form. When we respond to Jesus, we allow his Spirit to enter our lives. And gradually that Spirit will, as we saw in chapter one, repel the forces of evil habit in our lives. "So now the fair claims of God's standards can be achieved in us, if we do not live with the self in control but with the Spirit."[7] Paul knows what a battlefield his life has become since he declared himself a follower of Jesus. "I love to do God's will so far as my new nature is concerned, but there is something else deep within me, in my lower nature, that is at war with my mind and wins the fight and makes me a slave to the sin that is still within me."[8] That is the problem. God does not remove the tendency to evil which lies deeply entwined with the very roots of our nature as human beings. But he does give us his Holy Spirit to combat it. Jesus Christ was always victorious in his battle with evil, facing it as he did continuously through his life, and supremely in the crisis of the cross. He was the conqueror, all along the line. And the Holy Spirit is given us in order, among other things, to work out in us Christ's victory over evil. "Who will free me from my slavery to this deadly lower nature?" cries Paul. "Thank God, it has been done by Jesus Christ our Lord. He has set me free."[9]

Yes, he has broken the back of evil. He pioneered the way. He sets us free from condemnation, free from despair, to enable us to fight evil. And we fight (if we are wise) not in our own strength, but in his. When tempted, we should look to his Holy Spirit who lives inside us, and say, "Lord, please give me your self-control, your generosity, your peace of mind (or whatever it is) *now*." And he will. You will find that, like St. Paul, you will be able to say, "The power of the life-giving Spirit of Christ has freed me from the vicious circle of sin and death."[10]

Not let us make two things very clear about this life-changing power of the Spirit. In the first place, the change doesn't happen automatically. In the second place, it doesn't happen overnight.

Change doesn't happen automatically

The Spirit of Jesus isn't going to force change on you. He didn't force his way into your life, did he? Well, he won't force you to go his way. If you determine to hold on to some evil habit, he will not stop you. It just grieves him very much. He will reluctantly not be able to use you as fully as he wants. But he is love. And love never forces itself on the beloved. I remember asking a wise Christian in the early days of my Christian life why I could not get power over one particular thing in my life, although I had seen Christ clean up a number of other areas. He asked me, "Did you *want* his power, Michael?" Of course, I had to admit that I did not; I wanted to go my own way. Sadly, the Lord would not stop me. So be very clear about this. Christ can and will deliver you from any evil habit. He can do it at once. *But you have to be willing to let him!* That's the rub. When you are willing, his power is a reality which nobody can deny.

There is a very interesting example of this in the area of drug addiction. Back in the early 1970s, at the Second International Symposium on Drug Abuse, Frank Wilson, one of the six British delegates, listened to the learned papers being read on the virtual impossibility of keeping real hard-liners off drugs once they left the hospital. Then he quietly informed them of the sixty per cent success rate sustained over five years in his explicitly Christian rehabilitation unit at Northwick Park. It certainly raised some eyebrows. Much the same reaction followed a few years later when David Wilkerson, of *The Cross and the Switchblade* fame, was able to show a professional body in the U.S.A. that by means of full-blooded conversion to Christ and filling with the Holy Spirit he had been able to record a success rate among hardened dope users five times that of any secular agency. The point is inescapable. Christ can transform cases that would otherwise be hopeless. His power can change intractable habits in any one of us.

We all know what the expulsive power of a new affection can do: it can make the teenager forget his motorbike if once the girl of his dreams really crosses his path! Well, once a man has Christ inside him, he can discover a power to set him free from his own worst nature. "I can do everything God asks me to with the help of Christ who gives me the power."[11] claimed Paul. And you and I can know it too.

Change doesn't happen overnight

Secondly, beware of thinking you will become Christlike overnight. You won't. Some habits will be very reluctant to give way, just as some ice is so thick that it takes a long time to be thawed out by the warmth of the sun. And even though we may experience immediate deliverance from any particular wrong thing that is getting us down, we will then merely be ready for God to show us something else in our life that needs attention. The process of refining will go on all through our lives. We shall need time if we are to grow like Jesus. It is a slow process, just like growing a good fruit tree.

Have you ever planted an orchard? Then you know how impatient you are for the young apple tree and the pear tree you put in to bear fruit? Not a sign of any yet. But there is life, and there is growth, and next year, perhaps . . . So be patient. Keep in close touch with the holy God who has called you. Study the life and teaching, the behavior and example of Jesus if you want to know how God wishes you to act and react in the pressures of everyday life. And ask the Holy Spirit who lives inside you to take control of your personality and make you progressively more and more like Jesus.

There is a lovely promise in Paul's second letter to the Corinthians which speaks of the Holy Spirit changing us from one degree of Christ-reflectingness to another as we live in conscious and constant companionship with him. [12] We won't notice it, but others will. It was said of the early disciples that men observing them "were astonished and they took note that these men had been with Jesus."[13] That is God's strategy. He wants to take men, any men who are humble enough to say sorry and come to him in simple trust; he wants to rehabilitate them and show out in their changed character what he can achieve even in spoiled human lives when once he is given a chance. That is the strategy, and that is the perspective from which to plan your Christian life. Nobody will believe you have a new life unless they see a new lifestyle. And when they do see it, they'll be ready to listen about the new life—not before.

Notes

1. Amos 5:8
2. Amos 5:21-24
3. Amos 4:1
4. 1 Peter 1:16 (NIV)
5. 1 Peter 2:21-23 (LB)
6. 1 Thessalonians 4:3, 8 (LB)
7. Romans 8:4
8. Romans 7:22-23 (LB)
9. Romans 7:25 (LB)
10. Romans 8:2 (LB)
11. Philippians 4:13 (LB)
12. 2 Corinthians 3:18
13. Acts 4:13 (NIV)

4
A TRANSFORMING
FRIENDSHIP

One of the most staggering statements in the Bible is contained in the simple words of Jesus: "I have not called you servants. I have called you friends."[1] Jesus, who shares God's very nature, Jesus who was God's agent in creation, Jesus at once the origin, goal and sustainer of the entire universe—Jesus is prepared to call us friends. Friends, when we have disobeyed him. Friends, when we have been rebels. It is an amazing offer.

Pie in the sky?

When we commit our lives to Christ we begin with him a life of friendship which is meant to go on and get richer and deeper until our dying day. And then we shall see him face to face, and it will be wonderful. The one I now know by faith I shall then see. The one I fitfully love I shall be united to forever. "In your presence is fullness of joy, and at your right hand are pleasures for evermore,"[2] sang the psalmist; and I believe it. If the first installment of life with Christ here on earth brings such joy and fulfillment, there is every reason to believe him when he promises that the climax of it all after this life is over will be infinitely satisfying. This means that I can see my life steadily and see it whole; as a friendship from now on with Christ who will stick with me, change me and in the end receive me into his presence. Now notice two things about this Christian hope. It is not pie in the sky when you die. The pie, or a great deal of it, is available as we enjoy the Lord's company day by day. It would be infinitely worthwhile even if this life were all there is. But Jesus has said that this life is not all there is, and he has backed up his words with the resurrection. I'm prepared to take it from him. He has penetrated beyond the bounds of death. He knows.

Rewards and punishments?

No, it is not pie in the sky when you die; nor is it a refined form of selfishness to look forward to heaven. I do not love my Lord Jesus because I fear hell (though I believe that without Christ hell is my portion). I do not love him because I want to go to heaven (I don't, if he is not there. Endless existence would be exceedingly tedious and unattractive). I love him because he went to that cross for me, because he patiently waited until I was willing to make room in my crowded life for him. I love him because he is so patient with me when I am such a poor follower of his. That is why I love him. The thought of reward does not play any significant part in my motivation as a Christian. Nevertheless, I believe him when he says that "There are many homes up there where my Father lives . . . When everything is ready, then I will come and get you, so that you can always be with me where I am. If this weren't so, I would tell you plainly."[3] I believe in heaven, in short, because Jesus taught it, and I trust him. If he says our friendship is too precious for him to scrap it at death, that is good enough for me. It is wonderfully generous of him to be willing to go on sharing his new life with us forever. Yet it's just like him—his name is love.

Growing old with Christ

But this chapter is not about heaven and the ultimate enjoyment of his friendship there, though I think we should lift up our eyes from time to time to the future God has promised us. It is a wonderful thing to recall that life is not slipping away from us as our physical powers decay: we are getting nearer the day when we shall enjoy Christ's loving companionship to the full. And that has an enriching and broadening effect upon the character. One old Christian man, when asked his age, replied with a smile, "The bright side of seventy." He knew what he was talking about. That is why for the Christian old age is not an unmitigated menace, nor is death the worst thing that can befall him. As St. Paul contemplated the process of aging and the approach of death, he wrote,

> We never give up. For though our bodies are dying, our inner strength in the Lord is growing every day. These troubles and sufferings of ours are, after all, quite small and won't last very long. Yet this short time of distress will result in God's richest blessing upon us for ever and ever . . . How weary we grow of our present bodies. That is why we look forward eagerly to the day when we shall have heavenly bodies which we shall put on like new clothes. We look forward with confidence to our heavenly bodies, realizing that every moment we spend in these earthly bodies is time spent away from our eternal home in heaven with Jesus.[4]

What man could write like that if he did not share the friendship of Christ now, and expect its consummation hereafter?

The supreme ambition

Yes, Christ is the friend who will receive us at the end of our lives, just as Christ was the friend who accepted us in the first place. The Christian life begins and ends with him. It is significant that St. Paul, who came to know Christ initially on the Damascus Road, should disclose, some quarter of a century later, what was his supreme ambition, in these words, "My aim is to know him."[5] *To know him:* that was the very center of Christian living for the great apostle. He knew him already, of course. He had known him over a quarter of a century in times of success and loneliness, elation and depression, in banquet hall and in the dungeon, on dry land and in shipwreck; and yet his aim was to know him better. Perhaps in that simple ambition we have plumbed the innermost secret of the greatness of St. Paul. Christ was his friend, and for that friend he was willing to work and to suffer, come what may. But most of all, he wanted to know him better. He would have approved of the famous prayer of Richard of Chichester:

> Thanks be to thee, my Lord Jesus Christ,
> For all the benefits thou has won for me,
> For all the pains and insults thou has
>   borne for me.
> O most merciful Redeemer, Friend and
>   Brother,
> May I know thee more clearly,
> Love thee more dearly,
> And follow thee more nearly
> For ever and ever.

The phone and the letter

But how are we to develop that friendship with the Lord? After all, we can't see him. How can you develop a friendship with someone you can't see?

There are basically two ways. People who love each other can keep in touch, when separated, by writing letters and by using the telephone. You should see our students making a bee-line for the letter rack in the morning, or lining up outside the phone booth in the evening. If I were insensitive enough to ask them why they should think it worthwhile being late for their breakfast because they were eagerly fingering through the pile of letters in the hope that she might have written; or if I were tactless enough to inquire whether the nightly phone call to some far away lady was worth the price of the call—the answer would be short and utterly sufficient. "Of course it's worth it. I love her."

It's like that with Christ. Before we came to know him we had no particular desire to get in touch even if we believed in his existence. But now that we know him and love him, it's different. We shall want to use the letter and the phone. It won't be a dreary rule that we have to keep in order to develop a friendship. It will be the most natural thing in the world, for we love him.

The open letter

Our Lord has in fact written an open letter to all members of his family. In it he tells them about himself, about his plans for their good, about successes and failures of past members of the family, about love and self-discipline, about the family characteristics and the resources available to all the members. There are promises to claim, commands to obey, advice to note, prayers to echo, as well as examples to follow and warnings to heed. Best of all, this time of reading the Bible will warm your heart with love for your beloved Friend, and strengthen your determination to please him in the affairs of that day. It will become an important part of your life, this reading of his letter. You will find, I think, that the Scriptures do not exaggerate when they describe their own function as food, without which we shall be defeated; as a mirror, for lack of which we shall fail to see what we really look like; as a lamp, to shed light on our path; as a fire, to warm our cold hearts when they lose their glow; and as a hammer to break the rock in pieces when we are being willfully disobedient.[6] This book contains God's message for men, brought to us by the human writers, themselves men who lived close enough to God to hear, assimilate and interpret his will.[7] If you want to grow in your friendship with your Lord, you simply cannot afford to neglect it.

Does it look as if I am legislating? As if being a Christian involves a series of rules, of which one of the most important is "Read your Bible daily"? No, that is not the case. There is no rule about it. But it stands to reason that if you love someone you will want to explore them fully; and if you can't see them and can only communicate with them by letter, then you don't find it any hardship to study the letters! Sometimes Christians have made a fetish of Bible reading. They have implied that unless you read it daily, and preferably before breakfast, you are going to make a mess of the day. Indeed they have implied you are on the road to spoiling your friendship with Jesus.

There is a general reaction in Christian circles these days against such legalism, and rightly so. Jesus is not so petty as to withdraw his friendship if we skip reading the Bible for a day, or two, or three. But if it is true that the Bible is one of the main sources of nourishment for the Christian (and it is), then ask yourself how well you would grow physically if you ate your meals at rare and irregular intervals? And if you react against "the morning hour" of traditional Christian devotion, ask yourself if it is because you are really at your best for your Friend later in the day, say in the evening—in which case, fine. Have it in the evening. Or is it because you are too idle to get up in the morning? It may be a curious coincidence, but most great men of God in the past have found that if they didn't make time for Bible reading at the beginning of the day (for however short a time) they didn't make time at all. The rest of the day somehow seems to slip away. But you may be different. You may be iron-willed. You may be a busy housewife who can get alone for half an hour after your husband and the kids have gone off in the post-breakfast exodus. You may be the type that wakes up at night, and is able to guard the last half hour of the day for being alone with your Friend. Get a time that suits you, and keep that special for him. The important thing is that you should really *meet* with your Lord, not where or when you do it, or how long you spend at it.

How to begin

Do you wonder "How am I to set about it?" Perhaps the best advice would be to seek out a Christian friend and ask his help in learning how to read a passage devotionally. It would be a good idea to meet him once a week for, say, a couple of months, so that together you can study some chapters of the Bible that bear on the major aspects of Christian living. For instance, Luke 11:1-13 is a splendid passage on prayer, Ephesians 4:17-5:1 on Christian living, Romans 12 on Christian service. In such a regular, relaxed, weekly meeting you can share with him the many teething troubles that come up in the early days of every Christian's experience. He has almost certainly had similar problems to face, and is sure to be delighted to give you a hand. I personally found this weekly session with a more experienced Christian friend more help than anything else in developing my friendship with Christ.

But if no such friend is available, don't be discouraged. You have at your side one who will "never fail you nor forsake you." "You need no other teacher," wrote St. John, "for he teaches you all things, and he is the Truth."[8] I would advise you to get a good modern translation of the Bible. There are lots of them, though increasingly *The New International Version* is winning world—wide acclaim for its mixture of accuracy and readability. You would also be wise to get a regular system of reading it, or you may otherwise start at the beginning and get bogged down in the Book of Numbers, or do a circular tour of your favorite passages! *The Soldier's Armory* is a very popular method of Bible reading devised by the Salvation Army, and the *Scripture Union* is a worldwide and interdenominational method of reading the Bible in short, manageable portions, with some helpful explanatory comment in the various series of notes that are issued. It would certainly be a help to begin with one of these systems.

But don't be afraid to change it later on if you feel in need of some variety. Perhaps branch out on your own. Sometimes you might read a whole book at a sitting: the Book of Jonah, maybe, if you are feeling rebellious; or Peter's first letter if you are going through tough times at work. Sometimes you might study a single verse intensively. For instance, John 3:16, perhaps the most famous verse in the Bible, tells us of man's great need: he is perishing, like a drowning man in a river. It speaks of God's great love: he gave Jesus to meet that need of men. And by the time you have dug into a verse like that, you will find you have learned it by heart, and that may well prove very useful to you later on when you are trying to help other people.

More ways than one
There are lots of other ways of Bible study. You can make a character study, and trace the references in the New Testament to a man like Demas who was at one stage a close and loyal friend of St. Paul, and subsequently abandoned him "out of love for this present world"; or Andrew who is mentioned only three times in the Gospel of John, but on each occasion he is introducing someone else to Jesus. Or take one of the great heroes of faith in the Old Testament like Abraham, and see how he faced the temptation to take the easy course for fear of looking odd, the temptations to selfishness, to self-pity and to water down God's promises. That man faced the very difficulties that come our way, and more. The way he trusted God long ago can inspire and teach us today.

Alternatively, you may study a theme: what the Bible has to say about money, work, marriage, faith or perhaps what was the message and what were the qualities of the early Christians who had such striking success in the ancient world. As a change, you could take a single chapter, and see what its main teaching is. Romans 8 is a grand chapter with its assurance about a Christian's past, his present and his future with Christ; so is 2 Timothy 2 with its seven distinctive word pictures of a Christian worker. Or you can trace a single significant word such as "inheritance," "faithful," or "able." I have discovered a great deal by investigating the Christian inheritance that God has provided, by considering areas where he is calling me to be faithful, and by reflecting on what he has pledged himself able to do in and through me.

These are some of the different ways in which you can study that inexhaustible book, the Bible. But whether you are doing some exploration on your own, or following a system like the *Scripture Union*, remember that you are coming to read the Bible for a quite specific purpose. For you it is not "The Bible as Literature" or "The Bible as History" or "Biblical Criticism." It is the Bible as God's love-letter to you. So come to him in prayer before you begin. Ask him to bring it alive for you as you read, and to speak to you through it. And then read it through, and through again, looking for a promise you can claim, a warning you can heed, an example you can follow, a prayer you can use or something you had never spotted before about your Lord and Friend.

Two-way traffic

This Bible-reading is no one-way traffic. You will want to pause to thank God for some new truth that has struck you; to adore him for some fresh insight into what he has done for you; to search your conscience over some requirement of his; to think out the implications of some promise you have read. Bible-reading, in fact, leads naturally into prayer. The reading of his letter drives you to pick up the phone of prayer.

I once asked a student who had come to the Christian life only a month earlier, "What is the greatest difference you have noticed?" Her reply was interesting. "I have begun to love praying. I sometimes go on for ages, because I am really in touch." That girl had learned the meaning of prayer; it is talking with God. Talking with him about anything and everything of concern to us: friends, the job, time off, home relationships, future career, disappointments, joys, everything, including the day's timetable. Prayer is assuredly not a matter of set words (though there is a real place for formal prayers in a church service, so that all present can join in them) nor of fixed times (though without fixed times our praying will become spasmodic and probably chaotic). It is the sharing of our life with our Friend. Why do you think Christ died for us? To show us his love? Yes. To take responsibility for our sins? Yes. But supremely in order to share our life with us. "He died for us that . . . we may live together with him,"[9] with all the barriers formed by unforgiven sin knocked away, and with nothing between us to spoil the friendship.

The phone of prayer

The following letter came to me from a young woman who had been a dancer, a model, a nanny, and has subsequently married a clergyman! When she wrote it she had only been a Christian for a few months, and this is what prayer was beginning to mean to her.

> When I pray, it is to get close to God, to thank him for all he has given me and done for me, and to praise him in his glory. To ask for strength to do his will, so that through my actions people will see him in me. To get so close in the quietness of the mind that God can tell me what he wants me to do for him. To ask for help for myself and all my friends and family and for this world and its sin. To ask for forgiveness and strength not to sin again. To talk with my Friend and my God and tell him all my inner feelings that I could never share with anyone else.

A TRANSFORMING FRIENDSHIP

That is the essence of prayer: talking with God. But it involves listening to him, too. We aren't very good at this—at least I'm not. I tend to talk too much, and it is hard for him to make his will known to me. I was encouraged recently to see that I am not alone in this failure to listen, and Luci Shaw's poem which follows has challenged me to make more time for listening in my prayers.

On and off all day I've tried.
I can't get any answer.

Was I calling
a wrong number?
Is he out?
I'll try once more—
check in the big book—
dial, carefully.
A "busy" signal! Could
God have left his receiver
off the hook?

(Someone's at the door.
They'll have to wait.)
Dial "O."
"Operator—is this number
still in service? Yes?"
Spin it again. And still
no answer. I'm
positive my line's not
out of order. (Will
that knocking never stop?)

His phone rings on.
Easy for him to say "Need help?
Call on me any time!"
What if I can't get through?
What if he's gone?

or could that knocking be
him
calling on
me?

Yes, he may well be calling on you to visit that lonely person down the road, to take a bag of fresh fruit to that poor old thing in the mental hospital, or not to be impatient with your children. It may be that there is a gift of money he wants you to part with, or a word that would help the fellow you work alongside. So long as you will give him the chance by listening to him, it is up to him to get through to you, is it not? I find that comforting. It is his responsibility to show me his will. It is mine to do it.

Finding a structure

If you want a structure to build your prayers around, how about using the Lord's prayer as a pattern? After all, that's what it's meant for.[10]

"Our Father" . . . come to him with the confidence of children in the family and thank him for accepting you and making you welcome.

"Who art in heaven" . . . that keeps the perspective straight and stops us from getting over-familiar with God. He is great, glorious, heavenly: and I am puny, and should approach him not only with intimacy but with awe and reverence.

"Thy kingdom come" . . . pray for the extension of God's kingly rule in the lives of those in your circle (and wider) who do not give him their allegiance.

"Thy will be done" . . . pray for God's will to be done in the lives of those who do know him on earth, just as it is done in heaven. Here is the place to pray over the details of your day's agenda, to recall your special weaknesses and to pray for your church and your Christian friends, as well as those who are serving the Lord overseas, or seeking to extend his kingly rule in industry or in government.

"Give us today our daily bread" . . . Here you can include prayer for all your physical needs. God is concerned about them and invites you to make them known to him. The "daily bread" in what may have been the original Aramaic seems to have meant "the bread of tomorrow." Give us today a foretaste of the wedding feast in heaven! That takes up our physical needs but transcends them. It asks for all we need in order to spend our day as citizens of the Kingdom.

"Forgive us" . . . We never get past the need to ask for forgiveness from the daily sins and failures that all of us fall prey to. Call them to mind. Confess them. And receive his pardon. And remember, as Jesus told his followers, that you must be willing to forgive those who wrong you, if you are going to be able to enjoy God's pardon.

"Lead us" . . . How we need his guidance each day. Commit to him any special problem which is concerning you at present. Particularly anything that is going to "put you to the test."

"Deliver us" . . . from the unwelcome attacks of the evil one today: temper, greed, lack of self-control, or whatever your particular weak points may be.

For I am handing over to you the kingly rule in my life today, Lord. I am looking to you for the power to live as a Christian in today's world. And I promise that I will hand back the credit to you direct, and not take it for myself. "Thine is the kingdom, and the power and the glory for ever, Amen!"

Keeping it natural

This structure may well be a help in the special time you set aside for prayer. But friends do not only talk on fixed occasions! Christ is a friend, so turn to him at odd moments in the day. Is there some specially nice meal you have enjoyed? "Thank you, Lord," you say; and there's no need to shut your eyes or to kneel down in order to say it. Or is it some pressing temptation that attacks you? "Lord, please give me your strength." Or have you failed him? Don't wait until the evening to get it put right. Tell him at once. "Lord, I've let you down. I am so sorry. Please forgive me, and help me to learn from my mistake, and to ask you for your help in good time when I am tempted to repeat it."

One final thing. Friendship is all the more

delightful when shared. If you are out for the evening with some other Christians, why not spend a few minutes in prayer to the Lord before you break up? You are sure to feel shy to begin with, because it will seem strange to talk to God out loud in your own words in the company of others. But why not? Break the sound barrier: launch out, however haltingly, and you will not regret it. I think I get to a deeper level of fellowship with other Christians when praying with them in this way, than at any other time.

There it is then. Christ is your Friend. And friendships need to be cultivated. Make sure yours doesn't fall into disrepair through neglect. The letter and the phone are indispensable for absent friends if they are to keep in touch. And though the analogy is not exact (for Christ is not absent; he is wonderfully present with you always) nevertheless the point holds good. You *must* keep in touch with him and he with you, and the Bible and prayer are prime ways to do this.

Notes

1. John 15:15
2. Psalm 16:11
3. John 14:2, 3 (LB)
4. 2 Corinthians 4:16-17; 5:2, 6 (LB)
5. Philippians 3:10
6. 1 Peter 2:2, 2 Timothy 3:14-17, Ephesians 6:17, 2 Corinthians 3:18, Psalm 119:105, Jeremiah 23:29
7. 2 Peter 1:21
8. Hebrews 13:5, 1 John 2:27
9. 1 Thessalonians 5:10 (NIV)
10. Matthew 6:9, "Pray *like this* . . ."

5
A NEW ATTITUDE

In this age when we are more sensitive about freedom than almost any other subject, there are unmistakable signs that people remain in bondage. I received a letter from a man who was a habitual gambler. Even though it was wrecking his family life, even though it was driving him to bankruptcy, he could not stop it. He was enslaved. With you it may be something much less obvious than gambling. Swearing? Smoking? Alcohol? Drugs? Bad temper? Ambition? These things may begin like thin gossamer threads: but progressively they grip us, they inhibit our freedom and mold us into becoming the sort of people we don't want to be. We can't help ourselves. "The man who does wrong," said Jesus, "becomes a slave to wrong."[1]

Human nature hasn't changed since his day; we still please ourselves. However subtly it is dressed up, however various the guises it takes, self-centeredness is the motivating factor in human life. "Thank you very much," we say, "but I'll please myself."

The Bible writers were well aware of this universal tendency, and very honest about it. "At one time we too were foolish, disobedient, deceived and enslaved

67

by all kinds of passions and pleasures. We lived in malice and envy, being hated and hating one another."[2] That is Paul's summary of the governing factor in human attitudes before Christ comes on the scene. Hear Peter: he is writing about the paradoxical situation whereby the advocates of the permissive society in his day found their freedom shackled by the very things they allowed themselves. "The very teachers who offer this freedom from restraint are themselves enmeshed by evil habit. For a man is slave to whatever controls him."[3] Or notice the way James pitches into the rich and selfish monied classes of his day: "Look! The wages you failed to pay the workmen who mowed your fields are crying out against you. The cries of the harvesters have reached the ears of the Lord Almighty. You have lived on earth in luxury and self-indulgence. You have fattened yourselves in the day of slaughter."[4]

Yes, pleasure rules. Men remain now what they were then, "lovers of pleasure rather than lovers of God."[5] You, too, used to be like that, did you not?

But now you're a Christian. What is to be your governing attitude? Is it to be determined by endless rules? Ought you to go out and buy a textbook on Christian ethics? Should you be bound by the taboos of the Christian group you have become attached to? What is the right attitude for a Christian facing the practical and perplexing decisions of daily behavior?

A Christ-centered ethic

Mercifully the basic attitude is very simple indeed. Simple, but difficult. As ever, you find your example in Jesus. The supreme ambition of his life was to please his heavenly Father. Was it a question of the timing of his program? He waited till he was sure when the Father's "hour" had come. Was it the ultimate question of the manner of his death? "Not my will, but yours be done."[6]

"Christ did not please himself,"[7] said Paul, with masterly understatement. The implication for Christians is so obvious that it scarcely needs drawing. Our aim should be to please not ourselves, but him. He is like the general who has recruited us to his forces. "As Christ's soldier do not let yourself become distracted by worldly affairs, for then you cannot please the one who has enlisted you," said Paul.[8] When in doubt about the rightness of some course of action, "Each of us should please his neighbor for his good, to build him up."[9] The subject under discussion by St. Paul in that chapter is pretty remote: should Christians be vegetarians or not? The principle, however, is thoroughly apt and contemporary; we should please Christ, and act as his responsible agents in society.

And that is really all we need to know about Christian ethics! For we are not shackled to a code of conduct but are responsible to a person, Jesus Christ himself. Our motivation is not the stiff upper lip of duty, but the gratitude of those who have been set free. How does Paul pray for Christians at Colossae whom he has never seen? I guess he would pray for us in precisely the same terms, and it couldn't be bettered. "Ever since we first heard about you we have kept on praying and asking God to help you understand what he wants you to do; asking that the way you live will always please the Lord and honor him, so that you will always be doing good, kind things for other people while all the time you are learning to know God better and better."[10]

There in a nutshell you have the revolution that underlies all truly Christian behavior. My main ambition is no longer to please myself but to please him. Once pleasure was king. Now Jesus is king.

Just think for a moment what that involves.

The freedom it brings

It gives full play to our freedom. The church, alas, has not always been noted for its advocacy of freedom. It has been unduly conservative about its traditions, timid in allowing Christian people to use their heads, and not infrequently committed to policies of reaction

69

rather than reform. But when it has acted in this way it has done so in straight contradiction to the New Testament. There we read such sentiments as these: "So Christ has made us free! Now make sure you stay free and don't get tied up again in the chains of slavery to laws and ceremonies."[11] In this age which is dedicated to the pursuit of freedom, Jesus offers us the key to freedom we could never enjoy without him. A liberty to do what we know we ought; a liberty which is rooted deep within us as "the Spirit who brings new life in Christ sets us free from the downward pull of sin."[12]

The flexibility it gives

There's another advantage in this Christ-centered ethic. It gives great flexibility. It means we are not governed by a set of unfeeling, unbreakable rules which we must keep, but by a living, loving person whom we aim to please. The focus of behavior is not external to us, a code of conduct we are expected to live up to: it is internal, as the Holy Spirit first helps us to *want* to go Christ's way, and then enables us to work out that allegiance in the complexities of modern life.[13]

The reflection it demands

That leads to another important point. It means that you and I have to apply our *minds* to the question of behavior. There is no slick answer to what Christian action may be in any given circumstance. We can't even simply look at the New Testament and read the solution off the page. We need to see how the early Christians tried to please Christ in their day and situation, and then translate that attitude into today's terms.

This is even true of the Sermon on the Mount, where, if anywhere, Jesus seems to be laying down a new code of behavior for the members of the Kingdom of God. Is he not legislating? Not really. To be sure, he tells us that if a man hits us on one side of the face we should turn the other cheek. But are we to carry that out literally, without thinking about the principle behind it? If we actually do get clobbered by a man in a fit of temper, the fastest way to drive him really wild is to do a smart about-turn and offer him the other cheek. Literal obedience to the command could completely destroy the principle behind the command. The principle in this case is one of non-retaliation. Right. We must work out how best to show non-retaliation when we are provoked. But the ways of doing so will be legion, and may not include turning the other cheek literally at all! Thank God, we are not called to obey a code but to please a person. Fulfilling that aim will amply engage our mind, our will and our attitude to Christ.

The variety it allows

It also means that there will be a number of variations in the way Christians work out their faith in their life. Let nobody persuade you that there is only one Christian attitude to disputed issues. There may well be several. Thank goodness, God is not interested in dull uniformity. Return for a moment to the New Testament church and see how Paul handled diversity in Christian practice. Some of the Christians at Rome and Corinth would not eat meat that had been offered to idols for fear they should tacitly seem to condone idolatry. Others said, "It can't do any harm. These idols don't exist. We have one Lord and Master, and he has given us food for our good. I shall eat it and be grateful." Diversity in Christian practice, then, from people who interpret the will of the Lord differently on this matter. But notice how wisely Paul handles it:

> Don't criticize a brother Christian for having different ideas from yours about what is right and wrong. For instance, don't argue with him about whether or not to eat meat that has been offered to idols . . . Those who think it is all right to eat such meat must not look down on those who won't. And if you are one of those who won't, don't find fault with

those who do. For God has accepted them
to be his children. They are God's servants, not yours. They are responsible to
him, not to you.[14]

In point of fact, he goes on, God is pleased with both
attitudes, conscientiously held as they are. "The man
who eats meat eats it as a gift from the Lord, and he
thanks God for it. The man who refrains from eating
does so out of anxiety to please the Lord, and he too is
thankful."

What a splendid, liberal and responsible approach to ethics! Splendid because it is so humane.
Liberal, because it takes full account of the priceless
gift of Christian freedom. Responsible because it an-
chors Christian behavior in all its variety to pleasing
Jesus, the supreme pattern for human beings.

The joy it brings

Mention of Jesus reminds us that there is nothing cramping or burdensome about Christian morality. God does not want to make life dull and dreary for
us, but to make it full to the brim, and overflowing to
those who do not know him. To please him is not re-
stricting: on the contrary it is to take our proper place
in creation whose very existence is in order to fulfill
his will and do his pleasure. St. John's impression of
the song of the redeemed in heaven explicitly brings
this out:

You are worthy, our Lord and God,
to receive
glory and honor and power,
for you created all things,
and by your will they were created
and have their being.[15]

The will of God is nothing arbitrary: it is "good, pleasing and perfect."[16] Just because it is perfect, it is acceptable; we need not feel there is anything limiting in
seeking to follow that will. It is nothing less than the

very best purpose of God for us, the children he has brought into new life.

Such then, is the revolutionary attitude brought about by Jesus. Freedom from evil habit through the indwelling of the Liberator. Freedom from rules and regulations through loyalty to Jesus. Freedom from smugness about our achievements, both because no one can be smug about responding to love, and because there is still so much more to be attempted for him. Freedom from a critical attitude toward the way other Christians work out their obedience; remembering that they may discern the will of the Lord more clearly than ourselves, and that variety can be honoring to God providing it stems from a genuine desire to please Christ. Yes, the Christian ethic is certainly liberating.

That, then, is the proper attitude: to ask, "What would please Christ? What would he do in my situation? What action on my part is likely to bring credit to him?" Now let's be very practical and apply this principle to a single example, money. We'll look at a broader field in the next chapter.

The god of wealth

Money is god for a great many people. It is taken for granted that we should get as rich as we can, and that the more we have the happier we will be. An improved standard of living is the goal of political parties of the Right and of the Left. What difference is being a Christian going to mean in this highly sensitive area of money?

The Jesus we follow was remarkably unconcerned to acquire money. He appears to have been so poor that he had to borrow a coin when asked a question about tribute money; when required to pay it, he was glad to find a coin wedged in a fish's mouth. He was prepared to trust his heavenly Father for his needs. This did not mean that he was not equally prepared to work as a carpenter for his pay, and no doubt, to live off the proceeds of the catch when he went out with his fishermen friends. There was no doctrinaire opposition to money in Jesus of Nazareth; but no slavery to it, either. To be sure, he advised one rich young man to go and get rid of his cash; but he did not ask that of everybody. It is clear that money was standing between that man and discipleship. He was unwilling to let Jesus touch his pocket. And until he was allowed in there, Jesus could do nothing with that rich young ruler. "No one can serve two masters," as he said on another occasion: "You cannot serve both God and Money."[17]

The love of money

No, there is nothing wrong with money; but there is a great deal wrong with the love of money. The song was mistaken when it said, "Money is the root of all evil." That is a misquotation from the New Testament which says, "the love of money is a root of all kinds of evil."[18] A *root*, mark you; not the only one. And *the love of money*, not money itself. But think what a root of evil it is. Greed, oppression, avarice, dishonesty, fraud, robbery and often murder as well, all spring from this love of money. And there's a curious, twofold irony about it. First, money does not satisfy. As the Romans recognized long ago, money is like seawater: the more you have of it, the thirstier you get. And second, money does not last. Jesus spoke of the moth and rust that spoil the possessions of those who go for money on earth: today, income tax, inflation and the vagaries of the stock market replace moth and rust! But even if our fortune survives those hazards, it won't survive death. It is very short-lived. I remember talking to a woman who had nursed a man so rich that the ordinary cups in his house were made of silver. She discovered that it did not make him any the less miserable as he lay dying. The one certainty about our wealth is that we shall leave it all behind.

What, then is to be a responsible attitude for followers of Christ as regards our money?

Money—our goal?

First, we should not make money our goal. We shall remember the rich fool whose barns were so full that he could not get everything in. "I know what I'll do," he said, "I'll tear down my barns and build bigger ones! Then I'll have room enough. And I'll sit back and say to myself, 'Friend, you have enough stored away for years to come. Now take it easy! Wine, women and song for you!'" But God said to him, "You fool! Tonight you die. Then who will get it all?" Jesus concludes, "Yes, every man is a fool who gets rich on earth but not in heaven."[19]

Don't be a fool, will you? It is not crucial that you make that extra pile, or get that second car. It doesn't matter that Mrs. Jones has a deepfreeze and you don't. And please don't envy Bill's Jaguar; it is only a status symbol. Surely you aren't in need of any such boost to your ego. You may be poor all your days, but you are *rich*: you're heir to a kingdom.

Money—our security?

Second, we shall not trust in our money. This is one of the most insidious dangers in wealth. It tends to make men arrogant, independent and unwilling to rely on God for their needs. They have such a big bank balance they don't feel they need to trust anyone. And you don't have to be rich to trust in money. It's just as big a danger to the poor. They are tempted to feel that if only they had money all would be well, and they would have the security they have always lacked. Poor and rich alike need to remember that the Christian has one security only, God. In poverty or wealth I am his and he is mine, and that is enough. "Keep your lives free from the love of money and be content with what you have, because God has said, 'Never will I leave you; never will I forsake you,'"[20] writes the unknown author of the letter to Hebrew Christians. One Christian friend of mine, himself very poor, had his few choice possessions stolen from a friend's locked car. "No matter," he wrote. "They are welcome to my stuff. But praise God, they cannot take Jesus from me." And he meant it! I believe that if Christians were less attached to their possessions and more ready to trust God over their finances, the effect on society would be tremendous. It would stand out in such striking contrast to the prevailing attitudes on both sides of industry, and also to those of the man in the street.

I well remember a couple who came to Christian faith a few years ago. The man had just lost his job. The wife was unable to get municipal permission to start a play school, and they had a daughter who was declared to be dying. In addition they had to get out of their house. Their peace of mind, their trust in God over all this made an enormous impression on those of us who know them. The sheer joy they displayed as they trusted God in the dark was wonderful to see. And they were not disappointed. The daughter recovered; a new job was found; and they are happily engaged in helping to run a Children's Church. They have, in changed circumstances, proved the truth of the promise "my God will meet all your needs."[21]

Money—to get or to give?

Third, we shall want to give. This is all part of the inner revolution begun when the Spirit enters our lives. When Jesus was asked into the house of Zacchaeus, the notorious tax gatherer, the effect was electric. Zacchaeus was so magnetized by Christ's generosity that he said, "Sir, from now on I will give half my wealth to the poor, and if I find I have overcharged anyone on his taxes, I will penalize myself by giving him back four times as much." Jesus' comment is instructive: "This shows that salvation has come to this home today."[22] One of the yardsticks of a man's conversion is the change in his attitude to possessions.

Some years ago I was speaking at a conference in Jerusalem. One of the members had lost her luggage en route. In it she had packed a good deal of Christian literature written in both Hebrew and Arabic for free distribution in Jerusalem. Efforts to trace it failed until the last day, when it turned up damaged but with its contents intact. Indeed, there was one addition—a note from the thief who had stolen it. It read as follows:

> I stole this from you because I was a thief, but after reading your cards I decided that your way, the way of the Lord, was the only way. So I am returning this to you and returning to the ways of the Lord. You have blessed my soul, and I am now high on his way. Bless you.

I don't know whether that man had a sense of humor, but he added this slight misquotation from the Gospels to his letter of restitution:

> Seek and ye shall find.
> Take and ye shall receive.

Well, he had taken unlawfully, and had received far more than he ever imagined. So immediately it affected his attitude to money. No longer was it "finders keepers." Greed had been deposed by God in his life. The mark of a saved soul was a theft restored. It spoke volumes about the inner change in the man.

That, I suppose, is what Paul had in mind in these very illuminating words of advice to recent converts at Ephesus. "If anyone is stealing he must stop it and begin using those hands of his for honest work so that he can give to others in need."[23] The man whose philosophy had been "get" now begins to give. The man who stole from others because he had been too idle to work, now works in order to be able to give to others. How about that for a new attitude?

Money—our right?

Fourth, we shall see ourselves as accountable to God for our use of money. Hear Paul on the subject, who must have been rich at one stage or he could not have been a Roman citizen.

Tell those who are rich not to be proud and not to trust in their money, which will soon be gone, but their pride and trust should be in the living God who always richly gives us all we need for our enjoyment. Tell them to use their money to do good. They should be rich in good works and should give happily to those in need, always being ready to share with others whatever God has given them. By doing this they will be storing up real treasure for themselves in heaven—it is the only safe investment for eternity! And they will be living a fruitful Christian life down here as well.[24]

Whether I have a lot of money or a little is immaterial. As a Christian I ought to give a proportion of my income to God. The Jews used to give ten per cent, and I do not see how a Christian can give less (even if he is a pensioner or a student on a grant!). But characteristically the New Testament does not lay down any amount, or even any proportion. For giving is not so much a duty as a highly personal demonstration of our love to the Lord. Paul could write of the Christians in Macedonia, "Though they have been going through much trouble and hard times, they have mixed their wonderful joy with their deep poverty, and the result has been an overflow of giving to others. They gave not only what they could afford, but far more; and I can testify that they did it because they wanted to, not because of nagging on my part."[25] Naturally enough: "for you know the love and kindness of our Lord Jesus: though he was rich, yet to help you he became poor, so that you, through his poverty, might be rich."[26] That was Christ's attitude. Not surprising that it rubbed off on his followers.

It still does. I think of a schoolboy who loved the Lord, and gave up two-thirds of his weekly pocket money for Christian work. I think of a carpenter who had found Christ, and pressed a five-pound note into my hand at Christmas time shortly after his conversion. "Use it for the poor," he said. I think of an able young architectural student who celebrated his discovery of Christ by giving up his compulsive smoking and sending me a check to use in Christian work with the money thereby saved. Giving comes naturally to the heart that has responded to the giving of God. Too often church financial needs are tackled at the wrong level, it seems to me. "Give to save our old church" inspires nobody. But "Give because Christ gave himself for you" is a very different matter. The church to which I belong raises some 20,000 pounds on the annual Gift Day, quite apart from the regular collections and covenanted giving. How is it done? Not through large sums from a few rich individuals. But ordinary Christians who have found Christ give to Christ. Many of them give a week's income to that Gift Day; that's how it's done, and at least half of it goes to the church overseas.

Money for sharing?

Talking of overseas, one of the strongest ways of demonstrating the supra-national character of the Christian church is the loving contributions members make for our brother Christians in other parts of the world. Whenever there is a disaster, Christians are among the first to supply aid. Guatemala, Haiti, Bangladesh, Ethiopia, Poland, Uganda: in all these places Christians from other lands have put their money where their mouth is. It is impossible to neglect human need if you are a Christian. "If anyone has the world's goods" said St. John, "and sees his brother in need, yet closes his heart against him, how does God's love abide in him?" Nor is it necessary to leave Christian relief work to the official agencies like TEAR Fund and Christian Aid. Our own church in Oxford sent three of its members for preaching and teaching in Uganda; and they went with many hundreds of pounds of provisions and other necessities provided by the members of the congregation. On another occasion a single lady on a fixed income was so overwhelmed by the needs in Poland that she mobilized help from all over the city of Oxford, stored the provisions in the church building, and then took a convoy out to Poland herself. Money and possessions are for sharing.

Jesus had a special concern for the poor and needy. He told his followers that when they were meeting the needs of the sick and poor, the outcasts and the prisoners, they were in a very profound sense ministering to him.[27] The disciples took this to heart. The first Jewish Christians in Jerusalem were not too busy preaching Jesus as Messiah to organize relief for widows and orphans. The first Gentile Christians in Antioch were not too preoccupied with their extensive missionary work to mount a famine relief fund for their stricken brethren hundreds of miles away in Jerusalem.

It is an interesting and significant fact that the New Testament writers use the same word *koinōnia* for "fellowship" and for "financial contribution." The two are not unconnected! One of the most moving examples in recent years of Christians giving in order to express fellowship was in West Africa. There was civil war in Nigeria, and the Christians on both sides showed a love which transcended tribal loyalties and the peculiarly bitter feelings generated by civil strife. The moment the war ended Christians led the way in the generous giving and receiving of financial aid. Their nationalism said, "Hate the other side and show that hate by fighting." Their Christianity said, "Love the other side and show that love by giving." Their Christianity prevailed over their nationalism. Freely they had received from Christ. Freely they gave. That's what Jesus would do, isn't it?

And that's just the start

Let's leave the subject of money there, though the New Testament writers have a lot more to say about it—appropriately enough in view of its importance. They certainly do not share our coyness in talking about the proper use of money. They tell us, for instance, not to judge other people by their money and their clothes, and not to dress extravagantly or eat luxuriously ourselves when others are in need. They tell us that we have a responsibility to be scrupulously fair and generous toward any people we employ, remembering that we have an Employer in heaven. They tell us that we are duty bound to make provision for our family if humanly possible—remember how Jesus provided for his mother even when he was dying on the cross? Paul says bluntly, "If anyone does not provide for his relatives, and especially for his immediate family, he has denied the faith and is worse than an unbeliever."[28] They tell us that we can invest our money in lives by contributing to the cause of the gospel throughout the world. They remind us that not only the proportion of our income which we give directly to God belongs to him—so does the rest. How about your will, by the way? Are you planning to leave all your money to the family—or to leave some of it to Christian work? We are accountable to him for the way we use our money. It is only lent to us. We act as administrators of Another's possessions.

You see how the Lord refuses to be boxed away in one little corner of our lives labeled "religious"? He wants to lay his honest, loving, unselfish hand on the whole thing. Work out the details for yourself—such is your Christian freedom. I have certainly found it a rewarding and somewhat shattering experience to study what guidelines the New Testament has to give on this question of pleasing Christ in our financial affairs. But it is tremendously liberating to realize that all we have and are is his, and to use our resources deliberately and joyfully for him.

Of course there will be differences in the way Christians work out in practice that loyalty to Christ. There are no hard and fast rules. I think of one man who works in the stock exchange and yet is utterly surrendered to Christ in his use of money. I think of another who knows that for him financial obedience to Christ means having no assured income and working for a faith mission in the Philippines. In both men, despite the enormous differences, there is the same revolutionary principle at work: the principle of give, not get, of pleasing Christ, not self, in this matter of money. And that is what matters.

In this chapter I have taken money as just one example of the new attitude a Christian begins to adopt. But the principle of pleasing Christ applies equally to all the other areas of our lives. We shall be looking at three of them in the next chapter.

Notes

1. John 8:34
2. Titus 3:3 (NIV)
3. 2 Peter 2:19
4. James 5:4, 5 (NIV)
5. 2 Timothy 3:4 (NIV)
6. Luke 22:42
7. Romans 15:3 (NIV)
8. 2 Timothy 2:4
9. Romans 15:2 (NIV)
10. Colossians 1:9, 10 (LB)
11. Galatians 5:1 (LB)
12. Romans 8:2
13. Philippians 2:13
14. Romans 14:1-4 (LB)
15. Revelation 4:11 (NIV)
16. Romans 12:2 (NIV)
17. Matthew 6:24 (NIV)
18. 1 Timothy 6:10 (NIV)
19. Luke 12:16-21 (LB)
20. Hebrews 13:5 (NIV)
21. Philippians 4:19 (NIV)
22. Luke 19:1-9
23. Ephesians 4:28 (LB)
24. 1 Timothy 6:17-19 (LB)
25. 2 Corinthians 8:2, 3 (LB)
26. 2 Corinthians 8:9
27. Matthew 25:34-40
28. 1 Timothy 5:8 (NIV)

6
SILENT REVOLUTION

Some years ago I remember being struck by a remarkable film title. It was this: *Start the Revolution Without Me!* It seemed to me that the Christian life was the very opposite of this, and consists of the new believer saying to Christ, *"Start the Revolution Within Me!"* That is certainly what he does. It is a gradual revolution in most cases—no overnight coup. But over the course of a few years there is no doubt about it. We find we have been revolutionized inside.

We examined in the last chapter the basic Christian attitude of pleasing Christ. And we saw one example of the way this works out, in our finances. In this chapter we shall select three other important areas of life to illustrate something more of the change Christ makes.

How free is "free sex"?

Let's begin with the number one area where Christian behavior will run counter to the current of today's society. It is taken for granted these days that sexual love is the most important thing in life— perhaps the only thing that gives life meaning—and that we are entitled to pursue it as and where we can.

But even the advocates of free sex are finding that everything in the garden is not so lovely. For one thing, the pleasure doesn't last. Cohen put it very graphically in "Tonight will be fine":

> *. . . tonight will be fine—for a while*
> *Sometimes I see her undressing for me*
> *She is the soft naked baby love meant*
> *   her to be*
> *She is moving her body, so brave and so*
> *   free.*
> *If I've got to remember that's a fine*
> *   memory*
> *And I know from her eyes, and I know*
> *   from her smile*
> *That tonight will be fine—for a while.*

That's just the trouble. Tonight will be fine—*for a while.* Why, that's almost a modern translation of what the Good Book means by "the pleasure of sin—for a season." The trouble is that the act of sex is separated from a lasting relationship between the people involved. And that dehumanizes sex and demoralizes those who do it. Roger McGough has caught this spirit of bitter disillusionment on the morning after, in his poem "The Act of Love":

> *The Act of Love lies somewhere*
> *Between the belly and the mind*
> *I lost the love some time ago*
> *Now I've only the act to grind*
>
> *Brought her back from a party*
> *Don't bother swapping names*
> *Identity's not needed*
> *When you're only playing games*
>
> *High on bedroom darkness*
> *We endure the pantomime*
> *Ships that go bang in the night*
> *Run aground on the sands of time*
>
> *Saved in the nick of dawn*
> *It's cornflakes and then goodbye*

Another notch on the headboard
Another day wondering why

The Act of Love lies somewhere
Between the belly and the mind
I lost the love some time ago
Now I've only the act to grind

Of course, the unsatisfactory nature of mere physical sex is widely admitted by advocates of permissiveness. Robert Chartham in his sensational sex book *The Sensuous Couple* begins by maintaining that "physical sex should be a visible, tangible expression of the emotional love the partners have for one another," and, "If you make love only for the physical experience you are downgrading both yourself and your partner to the behavior of the barnyard." He protests that lovemaking should prevent you from being selfish. But the rest of the book goes on to talk blithely about the variety of partners emancipated lovers will have! What has happened to the unselfishness? The woman is jettisoned and another takes her place. For all his talk of considerateness for his partner, Chartham's sophisticated eroticism is just as selfish, just as sub-personal, as the quick job in the back of a car which he despises.

Christ's attitude

What would Christ say to all this? We are fortunately left in no doubt. He quotes the Old Testament on the whole purpose of marriage and sexuality. "Haven't you read . . . that at the beginning the Creator 'made them male and female,' and said, 'For this reason a man will leave his father and mother and be united to his wife, and the two will become one flesh'? So they are no longer two, but one."[1] In other words, marriage is for keeps, and God's intention is that the sex relationship should be the uniting bond between two partners throughout their married life. Fornication is out. Adultery is out. That is what Jesus stood for. That is what the early Church stood for. Christians are committed to it.

What's wrong with sex outside marriage?

Now why this very tough line? Because love, marriage and sex are meant to go together by the One who invented all three. Sexual intercourse is the closest possible relationship you can have with any other person, and the Maker's intention is that we use it as an outer symbol of the inner love we have for that other person: a love that, like God's own love, is fully personal, does not act selfishly and does not give up. What passes for love in these casual liaisons is often depersonalized, frequently selfish ("how much kick can I get out of it?") and normally short-lived, leaving behind it disillusionment and loneliness as the erstwhile partner is discarded on the human scrap heap.

What happens when the Maker's instructions are neglected? We have seen plenty of the bitter fruits of free sex in the past decade. It is a plain flouting of the will of God. It often produces unwanted pregnancies, divorce, abortions and V.D. It carries with it a sense of guilt. It frequently has to be covered up by lies and hypocrisy. It dehumanizes sex and makes it into an act in itself, separable both from a relationship and from a person. It causes traumas to the personality of those jettisoned, and a hardening in the attitudes of the "notch on the headboard" man. It artificially separates sex from love, fidelity, companionship and children. It takes something that can never be returned. It betrays an inability to control our instinctive drives. And it undermines trust. The man who cannot be trusted to master himself before marriage cannot be trusted to do so in marriage. Inevitably the girl he eventually marries (whom, hypocritically, he will expect to be a virgin!) will have to live with the gnawing doubt, "Will he remain faithful when my back is turned?" And what sort of a foundation for marriage is that?

Indeed, there are few things so disruptive of personality, home life and society as unrestrained libertinism. The Communists realize this. In answer to an enquiry as to what should be the Party's attitude towards the licentious productions being imported into Italy from the West, a directive was issued to the Italian Communist Party as follows:

> We are interested in encouraging this type of play, and are likewise prepared to praise actors of such plays as champions of artistic freedom. We want to encourage this sort of production, and must lead people on to produce others that are, sexually speaking, more daring still. As a tactical policy our aim is to defend an enterprise which is pornographic and entirely free from the restrictions of ordinary moral rules. The producers and actors are, in effect, like ants working voluntarily and without pay for us as they eat at the very roots of bourgeois society. Why should we stop them at their work?

It's not because Christians are against sex that they are hot on chastity before marriage and fidelity in it; on the contrary, it is because they value it so highly. Sex is too good a gift of God to cheapen. It is no mere animal coupling, but the deepest way in which two people can express mutual self-giving. It serves not only to symbolize but to deepen and enrich the unity and love between the partners. It is fun. It is satisfying. It is exhilarating. But take it away from the context of marriage and it becomes dishonest. For it isolates one type of unity, sexual unity, from the other areas of self-commitment that are meant to go with it. It is acting a lie. That is why the New Testament is so strongly against extra-marital sex. It separates what God has joined together—sex on the one hand, and lasting companionship, love and self-giving on the other.

Subsidiary questions

Once take your stand on this, and many of the other sexual questions are not so very difficult to answer. Should any variety of sex play be enjoyed by

Christian couples? Why not, within the marriage bond? How can any practice be wrong which deepens the delight of the couple in each other?

Should contraception be practiced? Why not, provided it is done within marriage, and responsibly in order to space children, not selfishly to avoid having them? Indeed, the appalling overpopulation of the world makes contraception no longer a questionable matter but a plain duty; we can thank God that just at the very moment in history when it has become so necessary, technical advance has made it so simple.

How about homosexuality? This is a highly complicated question requiring expert advice. If it is your problem, make sure that you get that advice from an experienced Christian doctor. The Bible is very clear that the practice of homosexuality is wrong, just as the practice of fornication is wrong. You may have a physical and psychological make-up which attracts you to members of your own sex in the same way that most people are attracted to the opposite sex. This problem can often respond to treatment. But it is possible for people with homosexual inclinations to refrain, through the power of Christ, from homosexual intercourse, just as it is possible for unmarried heterosexuals to abstain from heterosexual intercourse. You can't stop birds flying over your head, as the old Chinese proverb has it; but you can stop them nesting in your beard!

How about sexy literature and films? Erotic literature can be a cancerous growth in the mind. If you're one who suffers from vertigo, don't see how close you can get to the edge of the precipice. Steer well clear!

How about masturbation? This used to be the unmentionable sin of Victorian literature, the thing that sent you mad, the thing that could only be overcome by much exercise and cold baths. Now it is commonplace. What is the Christian, with his new attitude of pleasing Christ, to make of this? Well, on the one hand it is selfish, habit-forming and leaves you feeling rather dissatisfied and ashamed. On the other hand, it is nowhere expressly forbidden in Scripture, it has no lasting ill effects and is a much less harmful way of dealing with the overweening sexual urges of adolescence than sexual experimentation with others. Can you do it with an uncondemning conscience? That is the question. "Happy is the man who does not condemn himself for what he allows himself to do."[2] If not, it must go. And Christ the Liberator can break its grip.

Pornography

There remains that controversial matter of pornography. Controversial because nobody has succeeded in giving a foolproof definition of porn. Controversial because nobody can prove whether people are depraved by pornography, or go for it because they are depraved. Controversial because legislation against it would limit the liberty of the individual (though you have only to apply that argument to race relations to see the fallacy in it!). What is beyond controversy is that to separate sexuality as a sort of cult object, in isolation from lasting relationships and as the supreme goal of human desire, is out for the Christian. The Bishop of Stepney, Trevor Huddleston, put the Christian view very succinctly:

> The Christian religion takes its stand on the dignity of man, because it proclaims that man is made in the image and likeness of God. It goes even further than that. It proclaims that God himself has become man, and has, therefore, given a dignity to man which is infinite. Pornography is a symptom—it isn't a disease in itself. It is a symptom of a sick society. It's the consequence of society's thinking about the final end of man. It is the substitution of what, in truth, is the final end of man (namely the vision of God and the glory of God) by a limited and totally inadequate conception of what man is

> made for. Flowing from this real misun-
> derstanding of what man is created to be
> in this world, comes the idea that you can
> use the human body for a purpose which
> is wholly trivial. And this is what pornog-
> raphy does. Putting it crudely, you are
> substituting lust for love.

He continued the broadcast from which this quota-
tion is taken by calling on Christians to be prepared to
face the opposition this emphasis on chastity will
bring. "Marvel not if the world hates you. It hated me
before it hated you," was Jesus' comment on the inevitable difficulty of swimming against the current of
society which is at odds with God. Huddleston concluded, "In fact, purity of heart, chastity, lies at the
very center of the gospel, and if we preach the whole
gospel then we are bound to preach purity of heart."

With those courageous words we may fittingly
leave the subject of sex. I have spent an undue amount
of time on it—advisedly: it occupies a high place on
our interests, and it is one of the areas where the
Christian's determination to please Christ is going to
make him very different from his non-Christian
friends. It will spell nothing less than a silent revolution.

The problem of pain

If sex is the main preoccupation of our thoughts
when we are young, pain and death take over the top
positions when we grow old. Just as sex is regarded by
our society as the best thing in life, death is univer-
sally held to be the worst disaster that could overtake
us, and suffering the next worst.

One thing we can be sure of. Pain and death will
come our way. How does being a Christian alter our attitude to them? You have only to visit in a hospital to
hear questions like these: "Why should God allow it?"
We shall be better able to face suffering when it comes
if we have done a bit of thinking about it beforehand.

The problem of pain is an intractable one; nobody has gotten to the bottom of it, and nobody will. We need not, however, be too embarrassed by this. The Christian faith enables us to see suffering in a more positive light than any other religion or philosophy in the world.

Why does God allow it?

Let's be clear about this to start with. The Bible makes it very plain that God wants the utmost good for his creatures. Suffering and pain are never the direct will of God for us. He may permit them, but he does not send them. "He does not willingly bring affliction or grief to the children of men."[3] There are, however, four limitations on God's designs for our good.

First is the nature of our planet. It is consistent. It works to regular laws. And that is just as well, or we would never know where we were! But it means that if a knife will cut bread it will also cut my finger. The useful force of gravity which keeps me on this earth is not suspended for my benefit when I fall out of the window. So at least the possibility of pain is built into the very structure of our world where cause and effect prevail. This is inevitable; it is also invaluable. Pain can be nature's red light of warning. Were it not for the pain given by an inflamed appendix, it would burst inside you and you might die.

Second, there is the existence of Satan. The Bible is quite clear about the reality of this anti-God force, the devil, and I would have thought that there was plenty of evidence the world over to show that he is still in business. But the Bible is equally clear that the devil is not an equal and opposite figure to God. There is no dualism here. The devil remains "God's devil," as Luther called him. He is on a chain, albeit a long one. His eventual destiny is destruction, but in the meantime he is out to spoil God's world in every way possible. He spoils personal life by sin, family life by discord, social life by greed, national life by war— and physical life by disease. Although making it clear that individual illness is not necessarily the result of individual sin, Jesus left us in no doubt that the devil has a hand in disease. When he healed one woman on the Sabbath day, he referred to "the bondage in which Satan had held her for eighteen years."[4] And in the Acts we read of the way in which Jesus had healed "those who were oppressed by the devil."[5] This is one aspect of suffering we do well to take note of. There is a devil; and he is out to spoil.

Third, there is the fact of human free will. This is a major cause of pain in the world. God cannot take away from men their freedom when they use it to reject his way for them. That would be to reduce them to robots—and he is Love. Love can't be satisfied with robots. No, God will not intervene to stop train accidents, wars, thalidomide babies and the other products of man's misuse of his freedom. Let's make sure we don't blame God for these things.

But that does not cover all pain; it does not explain hurricanes and earthquakes, and there is therefore a fourth factor we must take into account. It is the interdependence of a fallen world. The world is not as God meant it to be. The Architect's plans have been scrapped by his clients. Chaos has resulted. And it affects every aspect of our rebel world. In the picturesque account of Genesis, man's disobedience results not only in his shame, his alienation from God and his banishment, but in the disruption of nature with thorns and thistles. Man and his environment belong together, as ecology is belatedly discovering. Human rebellion has affected our habitat. We are not just individuals: we are part of a common humanity, and it is tainted stock.

When you come to think of it, the sheer randomness with which suffering strikes is not so surprising after all. It is rather like smallpox. Once the virus has infected your bloodstream, the actual spots occur quite at random. There will be no rhyme or reason to their appearance. It is like that with suffering in the body of humanity. It does strike at random. It is no good asking, "Why should this happen to me?" any more than we ask with smallpox, "Why should this spot occur here?" In both instances the disease has to be met at its root. Suffering as a whole is linked with human sin as a whole; though individual suffering is not by any means necessarily related to individual sin.

What has God done about it?

Well, what has God done to meet the problem at its root? The cross is the deep and mysterious but wonderful answer. And from the cross there shine out these four beams of light upon our problem.

First, the cross shows that God is no stranger to pain. He does not allow us to go through what he himself avoids. He is the suffering God, the one whose royalty is displayed in suffering and in dying. "In all their affliction he was afflicted"[6] the Old Testament says of God, just as a father agonizes over a sick child or a teenager's wild oats. But supremely he shared our agony on that cross. The cross shows he knows all about suffering. The cross shows he has been through it. And he still suffers in and with all the suffering of humanity. Ever since the incarnation he has remained one of us. Isn't that just like God? He did not give us an answer to the problem of pain; he shared it. He did not explain it; he accepted it.

Second, the cross shows that God loves on through pain. If you are ever tempted to feel that suffering is a sign God does not love you, remember that Jesus died on a cross, yet God still loved him. It was into God's hand that Jesus committed his spirit. We can do the same, for we are not left desolate and unloved when we suffer. We may not understand the experience we are going through, but the cross of Jesus Christ assures us that God still loves us.

Third, the cross shows how God uses pain. Evil though it is, God makes good come out of suffering in a variety of ways. He does it in nature: think of the way an oyster uses the irritation of grit within the shell to turn it into a pearl. He does it in human character: think of qualities like courage, self-sacrifice and endurance which spring only from the soil of suffering. He does it in the spiritual life too. Sometimes he uses pain to *reach* us. I have met several folk who would never have stopped to listen to God and would never have come to know him, were it not for some tragedy that halted them in their tracks and made them think. Sometimes he uses pain to *teach* us. "Let God train you, for he is doing what any loving father does for his children. Whoever heard of a son who was never corrected? If God doesn't discipline you when you need it, as other fathers do, it suggests you are not his true children at all, but illegitimate!"[7] Sometimes he uses pain to *equip* us. Paul came to realize that a ghastly experience he had been through was intended by God to equip him to "comfort those in any trouble with the comfort we ourselves have received from God."[8] So just think of the wonderful way in which God blessed and overruled for good the tragic agony of the cross, and remember that he can and does use pain, though he does not will it.

Fourth, since the cross can never be separated from the resurrection, it points to God's triumph over pain. We have seen that pain as a whole is due to sin as a whole. On the cross Jesus dealt with sin at its root. He fought Satan and won. He bore sin and drew its fangs. He drained the cup of suffering and won through. Good Friday was followed by Easter Day. And we can look with sober confidence to a final triumph over pain because Christ has triumphed over sin which caused it. Paul does so in a famous chapter of his letter to the Romans:

> Since we are his children, we will share his treasures—for all God gives to his Son Jesus is now ours too. But if we are to share his glory, we must also share his suffering. Yet what we suffer now is nothing compared to the glory he will give us later. For all creation is waiting patiently and hopefully for that future day when

God will resurrect his children. For on that day thorns and thistles, sin, death, and decay—the things that overcame the world against its will at God's command—will all disappear, and the world around us will share in the glorious freedom from sin which God's children enjoy.

For we know that even the things of nature, like animals and plants, suffer in sickness and death as they await this great event. And even we Christians, although we have the Holy Spirit within us as a foretaste of future glory, also groan to be released from pain and suffering. We, too, wait anxiously for that day when God will give us our full rights as his children, including the new bodies he has promised us—bodies that will never be sick again and will never die.[9]

Such is the Christian hope. It is soundly based on the resurrection of Jesus Christ from the dead, the pledge of God's final triumph over sin and death.

A note of triumph

This means that we can face not only suffering but death in a new light. No longer will we see it as the worst thing that can befall us; no longer as the extinction of our lives. We shall see it rather as the door into a fuller life, a life which we shall continue to share with Christ as we share this life now. But a life which will not be marred by sorrow or suffering or decay. In his vision of heaven, St. John brings this point out with matchless poetry. "I heard a loud shout from the throne saying, 'Look, God shares his home with men. And he will live with them, and they will be his people and he will be their God. He will wipe away all tears from their eyes, and there shall be no more death, nor sorrow, nor crying, nor pain. All of that is gone forever.'"[10]

Away, then, with the gloom which so often

accompanies even Christian funerals. The Christian dead go to "be with Christ, which is better by far."[11] Let us wear boutonnieres—not black ties; and rejoice—not go around with hushed voices. Let those who have no hope of heaven, no expectation of life after death, treat death as the last enemy if they must. But for us it is a defeated enemy, ever since the first Easter Day. Of course there is shock. Of course there is loneliness for the one who is left. We must support bereaved people with great sensitivity. But for the departed Christian we can confidently rejoice. As Bunyan put it in his *Pilgrim's Progress,* when Christian passed over the river of death, "the trumpets sounded for him on the other side." Now we're Christians, let's have a bit more of that trumpet attitude as we grow older and face the somber realities of pain and death. We are the only people in the world who have something to shout about at this point. Our Lord Jesus has been through it all; he has overcome. And when we go through the valley of the shadow, he will be with us. He will receive us. He has promised.

Self-discipline

If the youthful years of our Christian lives show a silent revolution in our attitude to sex, and the later years lead to a similar revolution in our attitude to suffering and death, Christians are called to breast the current of popular attitudes in the matter of self-discipline all the way through their lives.

It is an unwelcome subject. "Do your own thing" is the accepted norm. But if we love him, we shall be prepared to do his thing. Self-control is really Christ-control, because I certainly can't control myself. I need him to do that. And in view of all he has done for me, I am prepared to let him do so. Let's have a quick look at some of the areas it may involve.

Ambition

Some people aren't worried by this one at all, but others are eaten up by it. They must get to the top of their particular tree whoever they have to tread on in getting there. Well, this attitude will change once we're Christians. In some ways it is no bad thing to have a driving ambition—provided it is redirected. I shall no longer be out to show how wonderful I am, but I can channel all that drive into living my life to the full for Christ. I think of a general, of a financier, of an actor, all of whom belong to Christ, all of whom have laid their careers at his feet, all of whom want above all to please him. Paul was like that. Once he had been ambitious for himself: now he was ambitious for Christ. Listen to him:

> I was a real Jew if ever there was one! What's more, I was a member of the Pharisees who demand the strictest obedience to every Jewish law and custom. And sincere? Yes, so much so that I greatly persecuted the church; and I tried to obey every Jewish rule and regulation right down to the very last point.
>
> But all these things that I once thought very worthwhile—now I've thrown them all away so that I can put my trust in Christ alone . . . I am bringing all my energies to bear on this one thing: Forgetting the past, and looking forward to what lies ahead, I strain to reach the end of the race and receive the prize for which God is calling us up to heaven because of what Christ Jesus did for us.[12]

Did you get that promotion? Then thank him for the wider opportunities of service it offers. Did you get passed over? Don't take it to heart. It means the Lord wants you where you are. You have only one life. You have given it over to him for his safe-keeping and his guidance. He knows what he is doing. He will give you the sphere of work in which the talents he has entrusted to you will be best deployed. So what are you worrying for? You don't have to prove anything by trying to show what a fine fellow you are. He has accepted you even though you are not nearly such a fine fellow as you thought. He has a place in his plan for you to work for him. So pray about your work. Tell him that you are willing to stay where you are or move on just as he wishes. You'll find that you are delivered at a stroke from the burning ambition that eats up some of your peers, and gives them a chip on the shoulder if they are not successful, or ulcers from overwork if they are. Make it your ambition to please him. Never seek, and never refuse a position of greater responsibility. Your life is in better hands than yours. He knows what you were made for, and he will give you fulfillment in your work.

Time

This is an area where we are incredibly wasteful. How much time do you simply waste each day? It must be phenomenal, even for busy people. I've caught myself at it even while writing this. I keep reaching for the knob of the radio to see how the tennis match is going! Of course, the Lord does not want us to be tense, over-earnest and killjoy, all work and no play. But he does want to guide us in the use of our time. After all, we have only the one life. Each day is an unrepeatable experience. He lends us our time just as he lends us our talents. And he wants to direct our use of it. Time for himself and deepening the friendship. Time for the job. Time for the family. Time for Christian service. Time for sleep is important: some of us have too much, some too little. Find what you need, and try to stick to it. There needs to be a balance, a wholeness about our use of time, so that we are not slothful on the one hand, or running around chasing the clock on the other. "My times are in your hands,"[13] wrote the psalmist. Let's ask his guidance on this important side of our lives every day, and his blessing on our use of it.

Leisure

This is worth a thought. The five-day week is universal. The four-day week is on the way. The amount of leisure will rocket. And masses of people won't know what to do with it. Stupefying boredom leaves millions gaping at the television for hours each evening. What will it be like in a few years' time?

But the Christian won't be bored. He shares his leisure time, just as he shares his work time, with his Lord. And there is always something to be done for others. I remember how in the last year of his long life the saintly Bishop Houghton told me that he walked down the road to the bus stop at eight o'clock every morning with a schoolboy who lived opposite—simply out of love for Jesus and the desire to share that love with the lad. That is the charm of the Christian life, or one of them. You never retire. You are never too old to be of use to your Friend . . . doing things for him, introducing others to him. The scope for Christian service in our leisure time is greater now than at any time in the history of the church.

Perhaps as a Christian you will want to review your holiday arrangements. More and more people spend an ever increasing amount on overseas holidays, when an equally restful time could be had nearer at hand at a quarter of the cost. At a time when world famine is greater than ever before, when missionary societies are more than ever pressed for funds, do we spend more on ourselves and our holiday arrangements than our Friend would wish? It may be worth talking over with him.

Smoke, drink and drugs

The older generation finds its escape route from the tension of modern life through alcohol and smoking. The younger generation is more addicted to drink and drug. What is a Christian to do about these stimulants?

Nobody should rob us of our personal freedom in these matters. We have been called to liberty, and this is not the moment to reach for the rule book. Nevertheless, two limitations on our freedom are clearly given in the New Testament. "'Everything is permissible for me'—but not everything is beneficial. 'Everything is permissible for me'—but I will not be mastered by anything."[14] That was one crucial question Paul asked himself: are these perfectly legitimate things going to rob me of my freedom by bringing me into a new bondage, by gripping me in a habit I can't break?

The second question is this: what effect will the exercise of my liberty have on other people who may look to me for an example? "But why," you may ask, "must I be guided and limited by what someone else thinks? If I can thank God for the food (Paul's example is drawn from whether to eat food that had been offered to idols, but the principle behind it is widely applicable) and enjoy it, why let someone spoil everything just because he thinks I am wrong?" "Well, I'll tell you why," says Paul, "It is because you must do everything for the glory of God, even your eating and drinking. So don't be a stumbling block to anyone, whether they are Jews or Gentiles or Christians. That is the plan I follow, too. I try to please everyone in everything I do, not doing what I like or what is best for me, but what is best for them, so that they may be saved."[15]

Now apply those two principles to drink and smoke and drugs. Are you master of them, or are they master of you? Spurgeon reckoned he could smoke the occasional cigar to the glory of God—but many Christians who smoke are enslaved by it. I suppose the Christian attitude here is either moderation or none at all. But then we have to take into account the second question: what would others think? Would it or would it not commend our Master? One friend to whom I was speaking recently told me that as a chain-smoking, hard-drinking man, he had cut it out completely when he became a Christian. On the building site where he worked they were amazed to find a real Christian. But having found him, they would have been even more amazed if he continued to drink and smoke. For him, therefore, it would have been wrong to continue. With you in your circumstances it may be different. It is something to put to Christ, and let him guide you.

It comes to this, really: where do you reckon to get your stimulus from? Christ—or drugs, alcohol and cigarettes? Liza Minelli rejects all drugs, including marijuana. "You know what I'm high on?" she asks. "I'm high on reality. That's what it's all about really, isn't it?" She is right. If we are high on reality, the reality of Christ as our friend, we shall certainly not allow ourselves to be enslaved by any of these things. We may occasionally use them when the circumstances are right. But we will derive our main stimulus from elsewhere. Listen to Paul again. "Don't drink too much wine, for many evils lie along that path; be filled instead with the Holy Spirit, and be controlled by him as you sing and make melody in your heart to the Lord."[16]

Language

"Men can train every kind of animal or bird that lives, but no human being can tame the tongue. It is always ready to pour out its deadly poison. Sometimes it praises our heavenly Father, and sometimes it breaks out into curses against men who are made in the likeness of God. And so blessing and cursing come pouring out of the same mouth. Dear brothers, surely this is not right!"[17] No, of course it is not. The cruel words, the foul talk, the backbiting, the white lies, the half truths and all the rest of it. Jesus Christ wants our language to bring credit to him. He is quite prepared to do the impossible and tame our tongue, if we will give it over to him. Paul expected to see the language of the converts at Ephesus change:

> Don't use bad language. Say only what is good and helpful to those you are talking to, and what will give them a blessing. Don't grieve the Holy Spirit. Put all bitterness, anger and bad temper away. Quarrelling, harsh words and malice should

have no place in your lives. Instead, be kind to each other, tender-hearted, forgiving one another, just as God, for Christ's sake, has forgiven you . . . Dirty stories, foul talk and coarse jokes—these are not for you. Instead, remind each other of God's goodness and be thankful.[18]

I like that last bit. Our minds are so constituted that we can't concentrate on two things at the same time. When the temptation to indulge in foul talk hits you, try thanking God for his goodness, and you'll find the temptation withers away. Another thing I have found helpful is to pray the psalmist's prayer before each day begins—as I climb into my clothes, maybe. "Set a guard over my mouth, O Lord; keep watch over the door of my lips."[19] You'll find he can tame even that intractable member, the tongue.

In all these areas of life the silent revolution goes on, once Jesus is welcomed into our lives and made at home. So long as we make it our determination to please him in all we do, we can safely leave the rest to him. He has the power to transform us, and transform us he will, provided we are willing to be changed. But not otherwise. He declines to force his way upon us if we refuse him entry to some area of our lives—if we say, in effect, "Start the revolution without me."

Notes

1. Matthew 19:4-6 (NIV)
2. Romans 14:22
3. Lamentations 3:33 (NIV)
4. Luke 13:16 (LB)
5. Acts 10:38 (NEB)
6. Isaiah 63:9 (KJV)
7. Hebrews 12:5-7
8. 2 Corinthians 1:4 (NIV)
9. Romans 8:17-23 (LB)
10. Revelation 21:3, 4

11. Philippians 1:23 (NIV)
12. Philippians 3:5-14 (LB)
    Psalm 31:15 (NIV)
14. 1 Corinthians 6:12 (NIV)
15. 1 Corinthians 10:29-33 (LB)
16. Ephesians 5:18, 19
17. James 3:7-10
18. Ephesians 4:29-5:4
19. Psalm 141:3 (NIV)

7
NEW RELATIONSHIPS

It was a hot afternoon, and I was watching the curate chat to the large number of elderly people who had gathered for their regular informal Thursday afternoon meeting. I was struck by the way he seemed to care. Then I met his wife, and I noticed their relaxed trust in one another and their obvious harmony. I remarked to my friend the vicar that he'd been blessed with a splendid new curate even if he was a bit older than most. Then he told me the story. Actually, I could not do better than give it to you in the curate's own words:

> When I was in my early thirties, I became involved with another woman. I fell deep into sin—sin of the ugliest kind— which made me reject all thoughts of God and which very nearly broke up our family life. Five months in a neuroses hospital under the care of some of the finest psychiatrists made no difference to my attitude to life. I came out of the hospital worse than when I went in. I had developed a terrible stammer; I took drugs at night to try to help me sleep; I took pep

pills during the day to try to keep me going; I went out of my way to avoid contact with anyone at all; I fainted in the streets and I jeered at anyone who tried to help me. I was determined to carry on with my selfish and sinful way of life, no matter what hurt it caused other people.

Then one Christmas, my son Alan (who was then just eight years old) gave me a picture of the Lord Jesus standing at the door knocking. "Behold, I stand at the door and knock; if anyone hears my voice and opens the door, I will come in to him and eat with him, and he with me" (Revelation 3:20). For a long time I deliberately turned away from that picture. But the knocking became more and more insistent until finally, at 10:00 p.m. on the 26th June, 1961, in utter desperation and almost unbelief, I said, "Lord, you say you can change people's lives—come into my heart and change mine." At last I had taken that step of faith, and immediately my prayer was answered. There was a complete transformation in my life from that moment onwards.

Undoubtedly there was. It was perfectly obvious, even to the casual observer. Once devoted to self, he was now an ordained minister, giving himself for others. Once ruining his family life by another woman, he was now happily reunited with his wife, and at one with her in the work of the Lord. Once dependent on drugs for excitement, he was now alive with Christ's joy and love. Quite a change. And nowhere greater than in his relationships with others. It doesn't take much imagination to think what a different place his home is, now. . . .

And home is the place to begin. Jesus once healed a man who had serious psychological trouble.

The man wanted to accompany him as a disciple on a roving ministry. In a way that would have been much easier for him. But Jesus said: "No. Go back home to your folks, and let them know what wonderful things the Lord has done for you."[1]

It's the life that counts

I don't think it is wise to *talk* too much about Jesus at home to begin with. They know you too well! They will probably think you have a touch of religious mania, and that given time it will blow over. So softly, softly, as far as talking goes. Begin with living. Let your allegiance to Jesus show itself in a new cheerfulness around the house, particularly when others are in the dumps. A new helpfulness when the wife is obviously getting tired—how about *you* doing the washing up and the cleaning and putting the kids to bed? Or maybe you are one of the youngsters in the family. One of the best things you can do is to see that your room is not so knee-deep in mess that mom can't get in to clean. "What, tidiness?" you say, "A bourgeois virtue." Not when someone else has to come and clean up after you. It is a matter of Christian consideration.

The scope for mutual consideration in the home is enormous. We are called to "Carry each other's burdens, and in this way you will fulfill the law of Christ."[2] Nowhere is burdenbearing more sorely needed than in the home. Think of ways in which you can work out in family life that principle of pleasing Christ which lies at the heart of Christian living.

New depth to sharing

If both partners in the home have come to know Christ, then this brings at once a new depth to their relationship. I vividly recall one evening a little while ago, when a couple—both of whom had given in to the claims of Jesus after a real struggle—said with tears of joy in their eyes: "This is more wonderful than our wedding day." At once they began to use their home for the Lord. They offered their place as a venue for one of the house meetings that was starting up in this parish, composed of some who had recently discovered the new life, and some who were still searching. It is a marvelous joy to use your home like that.

It is a wonderful thing for a Christian couple to go to sleep in each other's arms at night having just shared the events of the past day, its joys and failings, with the Lord, and having committed to him their lives and schedule for the morrow. It is a wonderful thing to be able to pray with your children—and they so often have a shrewder insight and clearer perception of right and wrong then we do. "Don't worry, Daddy," says my daughter when she sees my brow furrowed over some problem, "Can't you take it to the Lord? He will show you." She is right, of course! It has been well said that the family which prays together stays together. God cares very much about the family; he invented it. Moreover, it is the fundamental unit in society. What we do as a Christian family, therefore, is more important than any other Christian work we attempt for God. If we fail here, we fail comprehensively. Many Christians make the mistake of neglecting their family responsibilities, either as children or as parents, in the interests of Christian service outside the family. It's a snare and delusion. Don't fall for it!

Open house

A Christian family will be a happy place. Jesus is welcomed in, and "in his presence is fullness of joy." It will be a hospitable place: "given to hospitality" was one of the characteristics of the early Christians, and it still marks out authentic Christianity. Our home is not meant to be enjoyed in lonely isolation; it is there to be shared. This is hard work, but it is most rewarding, not only to the parents but also to the children. Once our daughter, aged three, went to stay with her Granny (who lives alone) and when Sunday lunch arrived, said: "I need more people." She wanted to know where the students were. When Granny replied that no students were to be had, she piped up: "Then let's go out and buy some!" That child had some root of

Christian hospitality planted firmly inside her!

I don't know what it is, but time and again people express their gratitude when they have been made to feel welcome in a Christian home. I would like to think it is something of the attractiveness of Jesus getting through. I remember an income tax inspector's home I used to go to when I was in the army. It was years ago now, but I have never forgotten it. This delightful Christian family used to open their home assiduously. If ever I wanted to help one of my army friends to find Christ, I used to take him for a meal and a chat there. They did not talk to him about Christ (unless he raised the subject) but their home radiated Christ's presence, softened him up and generally led him to ask what it was those people had!

No need to pretend

Of course there will be arguments and failures in the Christian home. But they won't last long, because as members of the heavenly Father's family they will quickly come to him and apologize and apologize to each other as well. "Do not let the sun go down while you are still angry" is sound Biblical wisdom.[3] It applies to husbands and wives (how can they pray together at night if they are holding something against the other?) and to parents and children. How important it is, by the way, that parents should not be too proud to apologize to their children. Yet too few do it. As Christians it will come naturally; we don't have to pretend we are better than anyone else. The fact that we have come to Christ for pardon means we are sinners, we know it, and are not ashamed to admit it to even our nearest and dearest.

Half-way house

But how about the situation when the home cannot be called Christian—when one partner is committed to Christ and the other is not? Tact, not talk, is the crucial thing. Don't be ashamed of your Friend, but don't embarrass others by constant reference to him. There's a lovely piece of advice, in Peter's first letter, for Christian wives married to unbelieving husbands. "Wives, fit in with your husbands' plans; for then if they refuse to listen when you talk to them about the Lord, they will be won by your respectful, pure behavior. Your godly lives will speak to them better than any words."[4] Above all, pray on for your loved ones. The fact that God has put you, a believer, in the same family as them is an indication that he wants to reach the whole family through you, his bridgehead. Your consistent life, your persistent prayer is likely in time to undermine the stoutest opposition. I met in Canada recently the tough head of a building firm—now a radiant Christian. But it had taken six years of wise, loving, prayerful behavior on his wife's part before he gave in to Jesus. Or think of St. Augustine—a licentious youth who traced his eventual conversion to the faithfulness of his mother's prayers. Pray on for those in your family who are strangers to Christ as yet. Ask him to shine through you as well as through your Christian friends who drop in. Expect things to happen. They will. I shall never forget meeting in Jerusalem an Arab girl who had been brought to Christ through the loving care of an Israeli Christian woman. The girl went back to her home, and said very little about her faith in Christ, but began to read the Bible and to pray. Her parents were curious to know what she was up to; they asked her; and before long they too had come to Christ.

Bleak House?

Some of you reading this may feel, "It's all very well talking about the married in their homes. I'm not married— and I haven't got a home." That may well be your position; but it needn't add up to a "Bleak House" situation. In the first place, remember that there are many things you can do, and many places you can go for Christ as a single person which would be out of the question if you were married. That is why Paul wrote to the Corinthians in praise of the single state: "An unmarried man can spend his time doing the Lord's work and thinking how to please him. But a married man can't do that so well; he has to think about his earthly responsibilities and how to please his wife."[5]

Second, it may very well be God's purpose for you to be married and have a home later on, but not just now. Can't you trust him to bring the right person across your path, without fretting because friends of your own age have their partners lined up? God's choicest gifts are for those who are prepared to wait.

But, third, it may be his will for you to be single. Paul wrote about "some to whom God gives the gift of husband or wife, and others to whom he gives the gift of being able to stay happily unmarried."[6] Both marriage and celibacy are a *gift* from the Lord. And though we would all naturally prefer the gift of marriage, that may not be God's perfect will for us. Jesus commended those who "have renounced marriage because of the kingdom of heaven."[7] That could be his calling for you. If it is, there is no need to lead an unfulfilled life. After all, Jesus remained a bachelor. Could anyone call him odd, unbalanced or unfulfilled? Several of my closest friends have remained unmarried for the Lord's sake, and their lives have been enriched by the sacrifice. Their hospitality to others and their talent for friendship have been enhanced by remaining single.

Others of my Christian friends have been bereaved at an early age, and have suddenly found themselves single again. This is how one young mother is coping, whose husband died five years ago from cancer at the age of about thirty:

> I'm getting used to having to make it on my own, and the Lord has been marvelously good to me. I have received so much in so many ways.
>
> I think now that I'm teaching, and I've joined the local choral society, I feel more of a complete person, if you see what I mean, though I still long for the day to day

companionship of give and take. But even there I think I'm slowly learning to lean on God more.

Here is another letter, which shows the courage of a young clergyman whose wife died from an overdose of sleeping tablets, taken during a deep fit of clinical depression to which she had been subject for some years. He has continued his parish, and writes:

> The Lord has been very real to me in the last few months, and the fellowship and hospitality of his people are absolutely wonderful. It is great to know it in experience as well as preach about it. This has been a year I will never forget, but one which I can look back on with thanksgiving as well as heartache. I'm indeed grateful for the advice to extract every positive aspect from the illness and passing of dear Jenny. With the Lord's help I am beginning to do just that. Life is very full, rich, and satisfying—as only the Christian ministry can be.

With Christ in the house it need not be bleak, even if, humanly speaking, you are on your own.

At work

It won't be long before the folk at work realize something has happened. They may wonder what makes you so happy even on a Monday morning. They may be amazed that you actually turn up on time, that you treat your secretary with courteous consideration and neither like a dictating machine on the one hand, nor a mistress on the other. You will get your leg pulled, and your good humor and patience will count for a lot. But you will be a marked man. They will expect from you a standard of behavior they do not expect from others. What a compliment that is to your Master! Your honesty in little things will be watched. Although the practice of "ripping things off" from the firm may be universal, although going home half an hour early when being paid overtime may be done by all the rest, it hardly squares with your Christian profession, and your friends will be quick to point this out.

Are you an employee? Then your attitude will be to do your job not just to get your paycheck or to keep on the right side of the boss; you will be working for Jesus, and you will want to turn out work of which he could be proud. Can you imagine any shoddy workmanship coming out of his carpentry shop in Nazareth? "You employees, put your backs into the job you do for your earthly employers, not only trying to please them when they are watching you, but all the time; do it willingly because of your love for the Lord and your desire to please him. Work hard and cheerfully in all you do, as men who are working for the Lord and not merely for the bosses, remembering that it is the Lord Christ who is going to pay you, giving you abundant wages from all he owns."[8]

Are you an employer? Then your attitude to your labor force will not be to see how much profit you can get out of them, and how cheaply you can make wage settlements. No, "you bosses must be scrupulously just and fair to all your employees. Always remember that you too have a Master in heaven."[9] When both sides of industry relate beyond themselves to the Lord and what he would want, then you get real harmony in a firm. But when he is left out of account, and rival policies of greed govern industrial relations, then it is not surprising that intransigence, suspicion and hostility are paramount.

Personal relationships at work are therefore tremendously important for the Christian. This does not mean that a Christian boss will never fire an employee. It does not mean that a Christian worker will never go on strike. But it does mean that the manager will be very careful to ensure that justice, not prejudice, is guiding his decision; and it does mean that the Christian worker will back the strike call not merely if it is popular but only if, in his judgment, it is just. However the complexities of Christian discipleship in an industrial society are worked out in the manager's office or the shop floor, the Christian in industry will have one overall purpose. He is there to work; to make his human contribution to the national economy—and in his work he will find a measure, at least, of his fulfillment as a man. But he is not merely there to work. He is there to work as an ambassador of Jesus Christ, and Jesus will be judged by his performance, to a very large extent—just as our country stands or falls, so far as its reputation in a foreign land goes, by the behavior of our representatives there. "We are ambassadors for Christ,"[10] claimed Paul; and very realistic he was. Because we are his representatives, his ambassadors, whether we like it or not. The question is, how well do we represent him? Our aim will be so to do our daily work as Christians that we bring credit to our Lord.

Concern for others

One of the most distinctive Christian qualities is love for other people. This sounds trite, but it is not. It is unique: so much so that the New Testament writers had to coin a new word for it. For it is an attitude which came into the world with Jesus Christ. The ancients knew all about philia, friendship, which was determined by mutual attraction, affection and respect of two people for each other—it depended upon the worthiness of the beloved. They also knew all about *eros*, passionate love, and rated it as highly as we do; here again, the worthiness of the beloved was crucial. But what Jesus brought with him was *agape*: and that love is determined by the generosity of the giver, not the worthiness of the object. Indeed, St. John tells us that God so loved the world (which he assuredly could not like, feel attracted to or respect—still less could he feel passionate emotion towards) that he gave his only Son for us. This love was sheer self-giving. It was not determined by the worthiness of the beloved but by the nature of the Lover. He loves us not because we are lovable but because he is love. His love, like his sun, shines equally upon the just and the unjust. Now that is the love which has reached us. That is the love which has taken root in us, and must get through us to others. Our lives are like heat pumps storing and reusing the heat generated by the boiler of his love. Therefore we shall care for people whether or not they are nice or attractive. We may not like them, but we shall love them, as he loves them through us. This means that we shall not rake over the coals the little man in the office who is the butt of everyone else; we shall not allow our weeds to blow into the next-door neighbor's garden however unneighborly he is towards us. We shall not write a man off because he went to a public school—or because he didn't. We shall not stick exclusively to people of our own social group or our own color. There will be no trace of snobbery or race discrimination in our behavior toward other people. God made them as they are. Christ loved them enough to die for them. And he wants to channel his love toward them through us.

Practical service

One of the ways you might consider showing this self-giving love for others, if you are young enough, is to offer to the Peace Corps or one of the missionary societies to go and work without pay for a year or two in a developing country overseas. You would be giving your youthful enthusiasm and such skills as you have, and you'd be doing it for Jesus. In the doing, you would be tremendously blessed and enriched youself. Even a short period is much better than nothing. Many of the students in the church where I work spend the summer vacation in some sort of voluntary service in a developing country. (Doctors in training do their electives in missionary hospitals.) Each year a number go and teach in Nigeria, evangelize with Operation Mobilization, or join up with one of the missionary societies for a couple of years. But you don't have to be young nor go overseas in order to find opportunities for service. There are plenty of them in your own town, your own street. The Lord will show you where you can be useful, if you are open to his suggestions.

Love in the church

There is one side to this love for others which is stressed above all else in the New Testament. It is the very special love Christians have for other members of the Lord's family. "Love of the brotherhood," they call it. It is a remarkable and most moving thing. I know nothing on earth to match it. The fact that the same Lord has loved you, the same Father accepted you into his family, the same Spirit lives in you, the same motivation grips you—why, this binds you to other members of the Jesus family wherever they may be, in a way no words can describe. I have experienced it in Cape Town and Nairobi, in Toronto and Hong Kong, in Sydney and Accra. It is a deep sense of mutual belonging to the Christian; it means you want to give to him; it means you love to pray together; it means the two of you are prepared to stand together even if to do so is politically dangerous, or socially frowned on. The church is no mere international organization; it is a supra-national organism. I shall have something more to say about it in the next chapter. All I want to point out at present is the need each individual Christian has for this society of Christ which transcends the barriers of race, age, class and color. You need the rest of the family, and they need you. Make sure that in your relationships at large you make time to develop a close fellowship with others who love your Lord, for the Christian life is not a solitary existence; it is a family affair. Perhaps there will be four or five of you Christians living in a flat; perhaps you may join one of the Christian communities to be found in many parts of the world these days. Perhaps it will be in the more ordinary shape of a church fellowship group. But do make sure you seek out the fellowship of other

Christians. It is vital if you are going to make s success of the Christian life. For as some wise man observed, Christianity which does not begin with the individual does not begin; but Christianity which ends with the individual ends.

Personal relationships for Christ

It goes without saying that the Christian will want his whole life to count for Jesus Christ. Magnetized by his love, we shall want to magnetize others. Let me make a few suggestions as to how we may go about this in our relationships with other people.

Demonstration method

Without doubt this is the most telling way of all. Our lives are very often the only gospel any of our friends will read, and if the writing they see there is unattractive, they won't want to know any more. On the other hand, if they are attracted by what they see, it will not be difficult to lead them to Jesus Christ, the author of the transformation which has impressed them. I remember an Olympic swimmer who, after a tough battle with herself, committed her life to Christ. She had been amazed by the Christian life of a friend of hers, and this disposed her to listen to the good news about Jesus.

You don't need to have been a Christian more than a few days to begin influencing people by this demonstration method. But it is sadly possible, if you cramp the Holy Spirit away in some forgotten corner of your life, to be a Christian of sorts for years without anybody noticing much difference or being attracted to Jesus Christ. And when that happens it is more than a tragedy. It is a slander on the name of Jesus.

Contribution method

There is another way in which we can help our friends, and those whom we don't even know. And that is by giving. It may be giving our time to planning a radio program or helping get a hall ready for a Christian meeting. It may be providing the refreshments at a home meeting. It may be giving our mind to planning an evangelistic meeting in the youth group. It may be buying Christian books to give or lend to others. One man wrote to me some time ago to say that he had come to faith largely through a Christian paperback. He wrote: "You may be amused to hear that when I told a friend of my conversion his comment was 'Oh, that's nothing. Old So-and-So found it so useful that he bought fifty copies to distribute to his friends!'" That man was using the contribution method in order to try to share his relationship with the Lord among his friends.

But the most obvious and basic aspect of the contribution method is straight giving. Giving to Christian enterprises that you know are committed to declaring the good news. This means informed, discriminating, prayerful giving. Jesus once spoke about a crooked business man who was discovered by his boss and fired. But before he left, he went to his boss's creditors and knocked their bills down for them. This meant, of course, that when he was kicked out, he had collected a number of addresses where he would be a welcome visitor, on account of the financial help he had given them. Jesus commended the man for his shrewdness (though not for his honesty!) and wished that Christians were as far seeing in their use of their money. "Make friends by the wise use of your money, so that when the day of money is over there will be people to welcome you into an eternal home,"[11] he said. In other words, invest cash in evangelism; through it some may hear and respond to the gospel, who would have remained ignorant of it had it not been for your sacrificial giving.

Subterranean method

There is a fascinating verse in Paul's second letter to the Corinthians where he invites their prayerful support for his work of making the gospel known. Literally he says: "You also helping together underneath in prayer."[12] What could he have in mind? I suggest that he is thinking of the fortresses which were such a common feature on the ancient world. Evangelism involves storming strongholds like that in people's lives. But a frontal assault is often useless. What is needed is a tunnel. That requires hard work, sustained work, team work. Such work is unseen and unsung. But it is crucial if the fortress is to be taken. Prayer is like that. It assails the inner recesses of a man's will in a way that all our talking cannot.

Now let me confess to you at once that I am not much good at this. By temperament I would much rather storm walls than tunnel away in prayer. But I know, I know from constant experience, that it is the tunnelling which counts. I recall vividly the mission to Cambridge University in February 1972. We had seen large numbers coming night after night, between eight hundred and twelve hundred. But there was not much to show for it in terms of definite conversions. We were driven back to the fundamentals, back to the tunnelling of prayer. Much of the last-but-one night of that mission was given to prayer by people all over Cambridge. On the final night of the mission we had a remarkable breakthrough by the Holy Spirit of God, and many people responded to Christ both then and in the weeks that followed. It taught men once again that prayer is perhaps the most important aspect of evangelism, and the one I, at any rate, am most liable to miss out on.

Invitation method

If one sixteen-year-old schoolboy had not used the invitation method with me, I very much doubt whether I would be writing this. He invited me to a meeting where I discovered what the Christian life was all about. As I went along regularly for many weeks, I observed the other teenagers at work on the demonstration method. And I know now that there were folk in the background tunnelling away on the subterranean method. These factors, under God's good hand, combined to bring me to my knees. My friend who invited me had only himself discovered Christ a few weeks previously. He was very inexperienced. But he could say "Come and see." And I shall always be thankful that he did.

That is precisely what you find people doing in the first chapter of St. John's Gospel. "Come and see." says Jesus to the first pair of disciples. One of them goes home in excitement and says, in effect, to his brother, Simon Peter, "Come and see." Shortly afterwards we come across a skeptical Nathanael: Philip counters his hesitations with precisely the same invitation, "Come and see."

The point is obvious enough. William Temple put it crisply. "It is quite futile saying to people 'Go to the Cross.' We must be able to say 'Come to the Cross.' And there are only two voices which can issue the invitation with effect. One is the voice of the sinless Redeemer, with which we cannot speak. And one is the voice of the forgiven sinner, who knows himself forgiven. That is our part." It does not require long experience. It does not require the ability to explain the good news. But it does require us to have found Jesus for ourselves. And it does require the desire to share him with others. Given those conditions, we will pluck up courage to ask people to the supper party, the house meeting, the church service, the rally or what-have-you where we know the gospel will be attractively and relevantly made known. The speaker on these occasions might be the Archangel Gabriel for all I care. He could do nothing whatsoever unless some faithful Christians had been doing a good job on the invitation method. And remember, they'll come if they like you, and if they respect you, and if they are impressed by the changes Christ has effected in you. But if they see no difference in you, they are not likely to respond to your invitation.

Testimonial method

It's not difficult to go one stage further than the invitation method, even when you are very green in the Christian life. It is to give Jesus a testimonial. To be willing to say, "Yes, there is a difference in my life, and it is due to Jesus. I have discovered that he is alive." Something quite simple like that. "Make Christ supreme in your heart, and then if anybody asks you the reason for your confident belief, be ready to tell him, and do it in a gentle and respectful way."[13] That was Simon Peter's advice—and he had had quite a bit of experience at it by the time he wrote those words. I love that passage in the story of the Samaritan woman who had encountered Jesus. She was so thrilled that she left her waterpot by the well (oblivious of the fact that she had come to draw water in the first place!), rushed back to the village and gave Jesus an open and glowing testimonial. "Come, see a man who told me everything I ever did," she said. "Could this be the Christ?" The men were impressed by her testimony. They determined to find out, and after Jesus had spent a couple of days in their village, they were convinced. "We no longer believe" they told the woman—and how she must have thrilled to see the fruit her testimony had borne—"just because of what you said; now we have heard for ourselves, and we know that this man really is the Savior of the world."[14]

It is difficult to overestimate the effectiveness of even the most halting testimonial to Jesus given by the most recent believer. In a parish meeting in East Anglia, one young man (a local villager to his toenails) who came from a grim home, was led to the Savior one Sunday morning. That same evening he had the courage to get up in church and say a single brief sentence, "I have today asked Jesus Christ into my life." They all knew him, of course. He worked in the nearby slaughterhouse. His words made more impact than the sermon; such is the power of the testimonial. It is available for every one of us to use.

Conversation method

How did Jesus reach men like Nicodemus or Zacchaeus? Not by preaching a sermon to them, but by engaging them naturally in conversation. This is something we shall want to become adept at. It is rewarding; it is stimulating; it is challenging and it is humbling. What a *reward* when you see someone else, perhaps someone whom you have prayed for and cared about for ages, commit his life to Jesus. What a *stimulus* to you mentally and spiritually, when you have to think your way around the gospel and the common objections to it, so as to be able to share it effectively when opportunity comes—and come it may, even when you sit down next to a stranger in the bus. The *challenge* comes from the complete honesty we must demonstrate—the willingness to strip away every shred of pretense, and to really put ourselves out for the other person, even if it means shortage of food or sleep, or months of waiting and battling in prayer. And it is *humbling*, because when you stop to think of it, it is just fantastic that God should use the likes of you and me to, as St. Paul put it "open blind eyes, to turn men from darkness to light and from the power of Satan to God."[15] But it happens. He does it, not you (once you start thinking you are rather a dab hand at this evangelism business you will be useless. God cannot and will not use a proud man). But although he does it, he expects the cooperation of our lips. The Lord of glory stoops to cooperate with us!

I always feel that a splendid object lesson in evangelism by conversation is given us by Philip, the business man from Caesarea turned evangelist. We find his story in Acts chapter 8. A modest fellow—why, he was the preacher in a great revival in Samaria; and yet, when he felt God was calling him to go down to the desert he went, even though there would have been red faces from his team when he failed to turn up to preach to the waiting hundreds that evening! God had a job for him; an appointment with a single individual, a black man in the desert.

Philip spotted this man riding in his chariot, and such was his enthusiasm that he *ran* after it. Just imagine him belting after a chariot in the desert at a temperature of 140 degrees in the sun! Had anyone been around to notice him, they would have thought he was mad. But he wasn't mad. He was obedient to the leading of God. And he found (as you will find) that God had already prepared the way. Of all incredible things, this Ethiopian in his chariot was reading not the *Jerusalem Echo* but the Book of Isaiah. Better still, he was reading that piece about the servant of the Lord who was led as a sheep to the slaughter and did not open his mouth before the shearers. What a chance! Even so Philip did not rush in tactlessly. He asked if he could be of any help to the gentleman. He asked if he could assist him over a difficulty he had with the meaning of the passage. Not surprisingly, he was invited into the chariot, and he began to tell the enquiring Ethiopian official about the Jesus to whom this prophecy looked forward. Before long the man professed his belief, and took the opportunity of being baptized at the only piece of water in that hot deserted Gaza strip—a spring that is still there today.

Now you and I won't expect to find people reading Isaiah 53 each time we talk to them! Nor will instant baptisms often occur. But if we ask our Friend to guide our conversations each day, and to give us opportunities to speak on his behalf when he wishes, then we are in for an exciting time. He will certainly take us at our word; opportunities will come our way. We shall fail sometimes. Sometimes we shall make a little headway. Sometimes we shall get stumped by a difficulty to which we do not know the answer, and we will have to go away and find out. Sometimes, however, we shall have the joy of leading an inquirer straight to Jesus personally. And I know no greater joy in life than that. It is the crowning thrill of using our relationships as channels of his love. And every Christian is meant to engage in it. Don't rob yourself of blessing by holding back!

Notes

1. Mark 5:19
2. Galatians 6:2 (NIV)
3. Ephesians 4:26
4. 1 Peter 3:1,2 (LB)
5. 1 Corinthians 7:32, 33
6. 1 Corinthians 7:7 (LB)
7. Matthew 19:12 (NIV)
8. Colossians 3:23, 24
9. Colossians 4:1
10. 2 Corinthians 5:20 (RSV)
11. Luke 16:9
12. 2 Corinthians 1:11
13. 1 Peter 3:15
14. John 4:29, 42 (NIV)
15. Acts 26:18

8
NEW SOCIETY

We have thought a good deal so far about the individual Christian. But God is not merely concerned with the salvation of the individual. He wants to forge new individuals together into a new community, which will in turn affect society, and indeed the very cosmos we live in.

I remember discussing with a director of the *Daily Mirror* the possible directions in which prevailing political tendencies might lead this country. He hoped that traditional British common sense would prevail, but he could not exclude the possibility of a totalitarian takeover either from the Left or from the Right. Since we discussed the matter, these possibilities have loomed larger. Economic policies directed towards the pursuit of profit have resulted in mass unemployment; and, in response, we have seen defiance of the law and politics by violence from the Left. There are plenty of countries in the world which display a totalitarian regime of a socialist type, such as Russia; or of a conservative type, such as South Africa. It could happen here.

What all totalitarian regimes try to do is to regiment people from the outside. Whether the method adopted be propaganda, repression or sanctions and incentives, the aim is to conform people to a predetermined pattern chosen by those in power.

What our Lord is seeking to do is quite different; it is to change people from the inside, and to do it not by constraint, nor by sanctions and incentives, but through setting them free from themselves and filling them with his love for others. His strategy is not to change society as such, but to change individuals, one by one; to change them from the inside and to unite them into a fellowship, so that they exercise a renewing influence on society.

Celestial strategy

When you commit yourself to Jesus Christ in personal allegiance, you join a worldwide family of those who have done the same thing. It is a family in which, according to the New Testament's very bold language, Jesus is the elder brother and we are adopted alongside him into God's household of faith. What a wonderful conception that is! No barriers of race, class, sex or age. That is what we are called into. Of course, we do not achieve it all at once. Indeed, we do not fully achieve it on this earth at all. But the whole thrust of New Testament ethics says to us, "Become in practice what in Christ you already are." You are sons—then live like that. You are justified—then live a just life. You are accepted in the Beloved—make sure you accept other members of the family.

That is the heavenly strategy. Alas, we often frustrate it by our selfish tactics, by allowing sectional or personal interests to motivate us. We close our ears to the needs of others, and remain silent when we should speak. But of the heavenly Father's plan there can be no doubt. He wants to show to the world, and indeed, Paul says, to the very angels (who have never known either the awfulness of sin or the wonder of forgiveness) what he can do with a community of people from every background and type, who commit themselves to him and allow him to shape their personal and corporate lives. "God has given me the wonderful privilege of telling everyone about this plan of his," said Paul. It is "to demonstrate to the heavenly beings how perfectly wise he is, when all his family—Jews and Gentiles alike—are seen to be joined together in his church."[1]

The Christian family

The church, then, is no optional extra for those who like that kind of thing. It is absolutely essential. Without it we shall not develop as Christians. Without it God's purpose will be frustrated. In the church of Christ there is available a quality of fellowship which will surpass any bonhomie you can find in the pub, or any community life shared by the dropouts. The Jesus Revolution showed this in the sixties both in America and other parts of the world. They were themselves members of the counterculture, people who had dropped out of conventional society. They had lived the hippy way with love as the ideal, along with free drugs, free sex and the lot. They had seen its weaknesses as well as its strengths. And then they became Christians. Soon they discovered what they were dimly groping for. Universal love began to become a reality for them. Free sex disappeared, and was replaced by a deep respect for brothers and sisters in the Lord's family; drugs, too, were discarded and replaced by a better stimulant, the joy which the Holy Spirit gives.

Of course this movement had serious dangers, which eventually overtook it. There was the danger of all belonging to one age group, coming from one culture and exhibiting one lifestyle. There was the danger of anti-intellectualism, and of becoming so estranged from the established churches that they failed to recognize their brotherhood with other members of the Christian family. The days of the Jesus Movement are over, but what a lot they had to teach the rest of us about real sharing, joyful, corporate witnessing to Christ, and a fellowship of men and women of different backgrounds and colors living together a clean, open, welcoming life, free from the grip of materialism. I experienced this style of life in North America, and was much moved by the quality of their fellowship and sharing. They knew what it was to *belong together* in the church. It was sad that, on the whole, the established churches had nothing much to do with this movement in its heyday, and this was reciprocated. In due course this imaginative movement disintegrated—back to straight society, or into heretical groupings like The Children of God.

At all events, the Jesus People demonstrated in a highly contemporary way the depth of fellowship and the corporate change of life which are fundamental to the church of Christ. Does the New Testament not talk about our all being sheep in the one flock, which Christ looks after and directs;[2] or stones in the one building which the Holy Spirit inhabits and shines out from?[3] Are we not branches in his vine,[4] soldiers in his army,[5] and incredible though it may seem, limbs in his body?[6] It is impossible to exaggerate the corporate nature of the Christian life. It stares at us from every page in the New Testament. It is through this corporate life, this new society, that Jesus wants to reach the millions who are strangers to him—not merely through the changes made in individual lives here and there.

Alas, many Christians have not seen this. I once talked to someone who had been a believer in Jesus and a fearless witness for him at work for three years without linking up with any Christian community. He realized what he had been missing; the church, too, had missed him. It is tragic when Christians fail to see that they belong together and need each other; as a result they tend to lose their zeal because of isolation, and the church loses their freshness and warmth.

The body of Christ

Think for a moment about that metaphor of the church being Christ's body on earth today. It speaks of the necessity and interdependence of all the different limbs in the body. It points to the harmony and unity of purpose that should characterize their relationships. It reminds us that all the members are at the disposal and direction of the mind; and that the mind can only express itself through the limbs. In other words, your ascended and invisible "mind," Jesus Christ, *needs* you, together with other members of the new society, in order to express himself to the world through the harmony and variety of the whole body's corporate life. If you are missing from your place in the family gatherings, then the whole family is impoverished and weakened. And so are you. Regular Christian companionship is absolutely necessary for mature Christian discipleship.

So join up with your local church if you have not already done so. Even if they seem a rum lot, you belong with them. By all means see what you can do to blow away the stuffiness. But you may well find that they have as much or more to give you as you have to give them. After all, they are more experienced members of the same family.

Church renewal

But what if the local church seems to you to be dying? You still belong, just as you do to the more antique members of your family, the great aunts and so on! It is very interesting to notice the way God has worked down through the ages. You can see it happening time and again in the history of Israel. God does not scrap his church when it goes down the drain (as it has made a habit of doing from time to time; it is composed, after all, of sinful men and women). He doesn't throw it aside and start again. No, as Jeremiah learned down in the potter's house, God is like a potter who remolds the lump of refractory clay when it gets spoiled.[7] He does not throw it away. The church of Ezekiel's day was like a valley full of the dry bones of a dead army. But God did not say, "Right, we'll start again." In his vision, Ezekiel saw God breathe his Spirit into those dry bones, and new life soon showed itself.[8] He continues to work like that. Perhaps he wants to use you, among others, to revive the sleepy church in your area. Time and again a church whose minister has lost his vision and whose congregation has lost what Keith Miller calls "the taste of new wine" has been revived by one or two people who mean business with God. They have not separated themselves from their local church in search of one more lovely miles away. They have heard the call to join God's people where they live, and their coming has meant renewal.

Of course, in the early days of your membership of the new society, you will be in great need of building up. Therefore you will be particularly dependent upon the warm fellowship and sound teaching of a church that knows how to care for new believers and how to build a community on the New Testament pattern. Perhaps you should go there once a week in order to show your colors! Then later you can transfer your regular membership to where it is most needed. God will show you, if you make it a matter of prayer. But don't be surprised if he calls you to join that branch of the family which is operating where you live. Give it a try, at all events; and get fully involved, not merely in public worship, but in the smaller, informal meetings appropriate to your age and particular interests.

The service Jesus left us

At the heart of Christian fellowship lies the Holy Communion, Eucharist, Mass, Lord's Supper—call it what you will. Incidentally, each of those names stresses one side of the central act of Christian devotion. "Holy Communion" reminds us that we come there in order to deepen our communion and fellowship with a holy God and with other members of his family. "Eucharist" means "thanksgiving" and warms our hearts with gratitude for all Christ has done to bring us into the family. "Mass" probably means either "meal" or "dismissal" of those who are not bap-

tized into Christ—this intimate family meal is for be-
lieving members of the family and none others. And
"Lord's Supper" reminds us who is the host and cele-
brant at that meal, Jesus himself, the one who inaugurated it at the last supper he had with his disciples
on earth.

We come then, looking back to the cross—the
cross he was going to when he had that supper with
them. He told them, as he broke the bread, that his
body would be broken for them; he told them, as he
distributed the cup, that his blood would be shed for
them.[9] It happened the very next day. How we need to
go back time and again to Calvary with grateful hearts
in order to reappropriate the forgiveness Christ won
for us there. That is where our adoption certificate
into the family was issued, where our citizen rights in
the new society were secured, at such tremendous
cost. The Communion awakens us afresh to the awfulness of sin, the greatness of his sacrifice and the
wonder of our forgiveness.

We should also approach the Communion with a
good long look at our own lives in the light of that love
of Christ's. How far do we come short of his considerateness, love, purity, and honesty? Now is the time to
search our consciences, get right with him, and as we
stretch out our empty hands for the bread and the
wine, symbols of his self-giving, to remember that we
are indeed empty in ourselves; we deserve no good
thing from God. We come simply by right of his generous free invitation to receive what he offers us—himself.

A third side to the Holy Communion is this. The
early Christians knew that "the Lord is at hand." It
was no festival in honor of a dead Jesus, but a meal of
companionship with a risen Lord. So thank him that
he is alive, that he is at work in you and the rest of the
community of the resurrection, as the church might
well be called. That is something to rejoice about.

Make a point, too, of looking around you. That
old lady, that rough shopkeeper, that lanky youth,

that black bus driver—you all belong together in the Lord's family. You all kneel or sit together to receive the bread and wine, the sacred emblems of his body and his blood given without distinction for you all. No place for pride before such self-giving love, is there? No need to have any chip on the shoulder! No excuse for keeping up a feud with any other member of the same family. You are all on a par: fellow-sinners, fellow-heirs of the same kingdom and fellow-guests at the same table.

And spare a thought for the future God has for his new society. It may not bring in Utopia on earth. God never said it would. But each Lord's Supper should have a touch of a future glory about it. It should remind us of the Marriage Supper of the Lamb (as the book of Revelation picturesquely calls it), the final consummation in joyous harmony of God's plan for all his people. *"Maranatha!"* cried the earliest Christians in their native Aramaic, when they sat at the Lord's Table. "O, Lord, come!"[10] It is as if they said, "Lord, you have come to this world, and lived and died for us. You have set us in this new society. We see many marks of your presence and of your renewing work. But, Lord, there's such a long way to go. Hasten the day when you wind up your plans for this world, and bring us all to the family table in heaven." No escapism there, you will notice. But just a foretaste of future glory to give us perspective in our daily work, and determination to be the best for him on earth.

Make room, then, for informal fellowship at home and at work; make room for meeting other Christians, especially on Sunday; make room for services of other kinds; but whatever you do, do not neglect the Holy Communion. It is the seal of your pardon, the food for your Christian life, the bond of your fellowship and a foretaste of heaven.

Corporate worship

While the Holy Communion is perhaps the most important act of Christian worship and fellowship—it was, after all, instituted by Christ himself—it is not the only one. The early Christians found it so important to meet together both formally and informally for mutual encouragement and service, for worship and prayer, for learning and sharing, that they broke the imperial law in order to do it, and were prepared to face execution rather than give it up. That is how highly they rated the fellowship of the new society. "We ought to see how each of us may best arouse others to love and active goodness, not staying away from church meetings, as some do, but rather encouraging one another, and all the more so as the day of Christ's return is drawing nearer."[11] Such was the advice given in the letter to the Hebrews. The quality of discipleship which that fellowship engendered captured the Roman world. Ancient paganism had nothing to compare with the loving, useful, happy lives of the Christian communities in their midst. And modern paganism has nothing to compare with it either.

But if the church is to make that kind of impact in society, its worship must have, and be seen to have, three qualities. Without them, what is done in church becomes as empty and meaningness as a shell when the nut has been removed. Worship must be united; it must be shared and relevant; and it must issue in practical goodness.

Genuine worship must be united. Naturally, for the various limbs in the body are stretching up in unison to praise and thank and trust and learn from their head. But if it is well known that the minister can't bear the organist, that the choir eats sweets and plays games through the sermon, that the congregation never talks to each other afterwards, and that the church council meetings always develop into an unholy squabble between the vicar and one of the parishioners—well, it is hardly surprising if such a church makes no headway in the neighborhood. It is useless preaching a gospel of reconciliation if it is perfectly obvious that the members of the church have not settled their differences. And that goes for

denominations as well as churches. We all know that
the Roman Catholics have for centuries unchurched
all other Christians, but are now changing their tune.
It has been equally true that many Protestants have
unchurched all Roman Catholics, and have thought it
imposible that anyone should continue a member of
that church once he had come to a living faith in
Jesus. This Protestant exclusivism is as wrong as the
Roman Catholic intransigence was. Every believer in
Jesus is baptized by the one Spirit into the one body of
Christ, in which there is no essential difference between Protestant and Roman Catholic, black or white,
New Yorker or Bostonian. Work for that unity in your
place of worship.

Real worship, then, must be united. It must also
be shared and relevant. The Lord does not expect us to
file into an ancient monument once a week, try to cope
with Elizabethan English, marvel at Gothic architec-
ture and a choir in resplendent clothes, and listen to a
professional in a dog collar. Where these conditions
still persist the church has to change. There needs to
be room for mutual enrichment and encouragement
of different members of the body. It simply will not do
for one member to monopolize the service. There has
to be room for the discussion of Christian principles
and their outworking in daily life, not just passive listening to a sermon from the preacher, however
talented he may be. (This is not to knock the sermon:
there must be proclamation of God's truth no less
than discussion of how to apply it. The two belong together.) There has to be informal discussion in the
small group as well as in the Sunday service, to enable
the members to get to know, trust and learn from one
another.

And real worship has to issue in "love and active
goodness," as the writer to the Hebrews reminds us,
genuine caring for the needs of society round about. It
may be the quiet visiting of the sick, or reading to shu-
tins. It may be mounting a campaign for better housing or for children's playing areas. "Fellowship is all

very well," remarked one friend to whom I showed this manuscript in an earlier draft, "but the dying, hungering, longing people on the housing estate or in the lecture room alongside me remain dying. We are damned if our lives are not pinned on that cross with our Lord. James rightly says that 'faith' alone is useless; faith is not faith when it draws back before the sacrificial giving of everything we have and are." He rightly points out the great disinclination to *work* among Christian people; we prefer to take refuge in a cosy little Bible study. But the two are intertwined. We shall only increase in understanding when we obey Christ, and engage in loving, active service for him. Otherwise we shall find dullness and apathy at the weekly Bible study, when the group meets and has to admit, "Sorry we haven't actually managed to be the hands and feet of Jesus today, but bless us all the same!" Genuine worship and genuine work go hand in hand. They cannot be separated if either is to remain healthy.

Is worship a priority in your church? Is it united? Is it relevant? Is it open for all to take a real part? Is it leading to action? If not, start stirring things up. It should be.

Club for non-members

The new society must never degenerate into an introspective club. It is, in the memorable words of Archbishop Temple, "the only society in the world which exists for the benefit of those who are not members."

Christians will therefore be concerned not only with evangelism, which we have considered in a previous chapter, but with social and political issues, with the equitable distribution of wealth and power, and the preservation of our world for future generations. There is a great deal which Christians can do in these areas. The church should assuredly not leave politics to the politicians or economics to the economists. The church at large and the individual Christian in particular may not be well equipped in any detail to pronounce on these highly complicated issues. But we all have some influence: we can stand up and speak up when the will of Christ is plain. It is our duty as Christian citizens. And in so doing we shall undoubtedly affect society. Let us take a glance at some of the crucial areas where as Christians we should be involved.

Social concern

I remember being delighted, on a visit to Australia, to discover the tremendous social conscience of the diocese of Sydney. This has the reputation of being the most uniformly evangelical diocese in the whole Anglican Communion. Far from evangelistic emphasis being the foe of social involvement, the reverse has proved to be the case. It gives more money to social work than any diocese in the world, and the motivation comes directly from a strong sense of the new life brought by Christ. Therefore *of course* the church must build hospitals for the aged, villages for the retired, homes for unmarried mothers, for boys and girls on probation and for when they come out of prison. *Of course* they must provide help for the down-and-outs and would-be suicides. It is as important as the missionary work in which they engage so wholeheartedly. Sydney's Archbishop Marcus Loane was a superb example of this balance. On the one hand, he had just walked the fabulously wild Kadoka Trail, a route through the mountains and jungles which had a gruesome reputation in the Second World War, in order to help raise a million dollars for the impoverished diocese of New Guinea. On the other, he had just fearlessly accused the Federal Government of policies which were producing a hundred thousand unemployed and family hardship hurting half a million. Angry questions were asked in Parliament. One member requested the archbishop to stick to sin while politicians handled economics. The Prime Minister patronizingly said he would have a chat with the archbishop, who clearly did not understand these things. The result? Churchmen at large backed the Christian lead given by Archbishop Loane, and all the other diocesan bishops backed him to the hilt, to the great embarrassment of a government which was unwilling to grapple with a crying social problem because of a forthcoming election. Christian concern over the unemployment issue led to a national inquiry into the causes and cure of poverty in Australia.

Race relations

In an era when race relations threaten to be a major disruptive force in the world, it is appropriate that the President of the World Council of Churches should be a West Indian, that the British Council of Churches should have been among the first to prepare a welcome and a home for the Asians deported from Uganda, and that the World Council of Churches should have initiated a major effort to combat racism. A good many years ago in America the Civil Rights Commission came out in support of black claims for equality in citizenship rights, and yet absolutely nothing was done to carry those recommendations through. The magnetic leadership of Martin Luther King, with his policy of non-violent protest allied to civil disobedience, forced both president and congress to act. Though assassinated in the cause of winning justice for blacks, Martin Luther King's life and ideals still live on and have an enormous influence for freedom and the dignity of man the world over. In his Christmas Eve broadcast shortly before he was killed, he outlined his vision for humanity. It shows not only the greatness of the man but the Christ-centered motivation for his social concern:

> I still have a dream this morning that one day every Negro in this country, every colored person in the world, will be judged on the basis of the content of his character rather than the color of his skin, and every man will respect the dignity and worth of human personality. I

still have a dream today that one day the idle industries of Appalachia will be revitalised and the empty stomachs of Mississippi will be filled, and brotherhood will be more than a few words at the end of a prayer, but rather the first item on every legislative agenda. I still have a dream today that one day justice will roll down like water, and righteousness like a mighty stream. I still have a dream today that in all of our state houses and city halls men will be elected to go there who will do justly, and love mercy and walk humbly with their God. I still have a dream today that one day war will come to an end, that men will beat their swords into plowshares and their spears into pruning hooks, that nations will no longer rise up against nations, neither will they study war any more. . . . I still have a dream that with this faith we shall be able to adjourn the councils of despair and bring new light into the dark chambers of pessimism. With this faith we will be able to speed up the day when there will be peace on earth and goodwill toward men. It will be a glorious day, the morning stars will sing together, and the sons of God will shout for joy.

Such was the vision behind the practical action of one of this century's truly great Christians. Yet he was shot. Does this mean that Christians are mistaken in renouncing force and rejecting violent revolution in a world that seems to be becoming increasingly violent?

Revolutionary violence

This is a difficult issue. It is hard, on the one hand, to see how the church, committed as it is to love and peace, could be involved in violence and revolution. But what is it to do, on the other hand, when the surrounding society is utterly corrupt, when justice has been banished, and oppression is the order of the day? The temptation to violence is almost irresistible in those circumstances, and yet for the life of me I cannot see violent revolution squaring with the example of Jesus. Though he had some Zealot revolutionaries among his disciples, he would not accept the option of violent revolution in the interests of either nation or ideology. Ironically enough, he was crucified as a revolutionary leader ("King of the Jews"), and yet he refused to allow the ideological cause of the Kingdom of God or the political cause of throwing off the Roman yoke to tempt him to sanction arms. Force is not exercised by force. Violence breeds violence. And that will give the Christian pause before considering it, even under extreme provocation. The cross of Jesus shows us clearly that violence is disarmed not by retaliation, but by patient, innocent suffering.

There have been Christians of the utmost spirituality and integrity who, goaded beyond endurance, have accepted the option of violence for the sake of helping other people whom it seemed impossible to defend in any other way. One thinks of Camilo Torres, the Roman Catholic priest who was so appalled at the conditions of the peasants in Colombia that he sided with the guerillas in the mountains in the attempt to improve their lot by violent revolution. This brave man joined the revolution out of love to his neighbor, and we must salute him. He was shot in action in 1966. And many Latin American billboards still carry the legend *Camilo viva!* Or one thinks of Dietrich Bonhoeffer, the lifelong Christian pacifist who eventually was so appalled by the atrocities of Hitler's Germany that he took part, out of Christian love for the German people, in an attempt to kill Hitler—and paid the extreme penalty. These great men reluctantly took the way of violence, but only when this evil (as they saw it to be) seemed less evil than the *status quo*. They may have been wrong. But we can certainly not judge

137

them. They had the courage to give practical proof of their sense of justice and their Christian love for others, knowing that they were risking their lives by so doing. Equally great men, such as Martin Luther King, Bishop Helder Camara in brazil and Bishop Wilson in a Japanese prisoner of war camp in World War Two, have followed Jesus in meeting violence by suffering, and in the long run their judgment may well prove the sounder. "Christians," said Jacques Ellul, at the end of his careful book, *Violence*, "will be sufficiently and completely present in the world if they suffer with those who suffer, if they seek out with those sufferers the one way of salvation, if they bear witness before God and man to the consequences of injustice and the proclamation of love."

Reactionary violence

But the Christian will not forget that there is a reactionary as well as a revolutionary violence. In the South American scene, revolutionary violence is understandably sparked off by the violent oppression, rapacity and ruthlessness of the tiny ruling class. In Brazil, for instance, ten percent of the population owns ninety percent of the land. Such conditions are ripe for revolution. What attitude is the Christian to adopt?

A French Canadian, Abbé Pierre, was visiting Uruguay and was asked on T.V. a loaded question about his attitude toward the guerillas. He replied, "Yes, I meet them sometimes. I listen to them. And when I have listened to them, I find I have nothing to say to them, because although I am not rich, I do know where the next meal is coming from. I have something to wear. I am not a father burdened with shame and humiliation because he has children he cannot feed. Is it for me to tell them 'Be patient a little longer' when I am perfectly well aware that for centuries their patience has been abused? I have nothing to say to them.

"What I am sure of, when I have listened to them,

is that I should rage, scream at those who accuse them, judge them, condemn them, those who have the lion's share on their plates, who have grabbed everything for themselves and have left everyone else's plate empty around them, and who with a kind expression on their faces will tell you, 'We are for peace.' I know that I ought to shout at them, 'Your privileges are based on theft. It is you who are the really violent ones, you who are the real killers.'"

Ecology

In recent years, leading scientists the world over have been warning us that unless we change our priorities radically, our world is heading for destruction within two generations. The threat to human survival comes from a variety of sources. There is the specter of the hydrogen bomb; and an increasing number of nations joins the Nuclear Club every year. There is the stockpiling by many nations of germ weapons which can wipe out a whole country overnight. There is the unsolved problem of hunger; nearly two-thirds of the world's population is underfed. There is the appalling threat of overpopulation. The world population took two centuries to double between the seventeenth and the nineteenth centuries. But now it doubles every thirty-five years! By the year two thousand there will be twice as many people on this over-crowded planet as there are now. Most of them will be born to starvation, since food supplies cannot even support the present population, and almost all the cultivable land in the world has already been used up. There are plenty of other problems. We are depleting the natural resources of our planet at an alarming rate. All known reserves of oil may well be used up in fifty years, and the same looks probable for the deposits of all but a few metals. Furthermore, the world is being polluted to an incredible extent. We are like rats, fouling our own cage. We pollute the atmosphere with carbon dioxide, poison the seas with oil, sewage and P.C.P.'s, and inundate the land with garbage, more and more of it indestructible plastic material. Add to this the gross inequality between the "Have's" and the "Have-nots" and the critical nature of the world situation comes into even sharper focus. An American in his lifetime eats fifty times more food than an Indian. He pollutes the environment fifty times as much as his Indian counterpart because of the industrialization of Western society. The inequality which exists between industralized and non-industrialized nations to so marked a degree is a massive irritant to war.

As Christians whose lot it is to live in such a significant and indeed terrible chapter of the world's history, how are we to carry out our Lord's command to love our neighbor? Bishop Hugh Montefiore of Birmingham, England, who has consistently pointed out the seriousness of these issues, wrote this adaptation of the Ten Commandments:

> *I am the Lord your God; you shall have no other gods but me.*
>
> *You shall not make to yourself any graven image or idol,* such as the Gross National Product or possessions or riches, *whether in the heavens above or in the earth beneath or in the waters under the earth: you shall not bow down and serve them.*
>
> *You shall not take the name of the Lord your God in vain* by calling on his name but ignoring his natural law.
>
> *Remember that you set apart* one day in a week for true festivity, or you will be bored stiff in the technological age you are bringing on yourselves.
>
> *Honor your father and mother,* but do not seek to prolong their natural term of life so that they are miserable.
>
> *You shall not murder* future generations by your present greed.

You shall not commit sexual sin by producing more children than is your right.

You shall not bear false witness against your overseas neighbors by lying to yourself about the extent of their need.

You shall not covet an ever increasing standard of living.

Secular assumptions—and Christian attitudes

As Christians we shall want to contest the assumptions of most of our contemporaries in the industrialized West; namely, that we have a right to an ever increasing standard of living, that increased wealth brings increased happiness, that governments should make material prosperity their chief aim and that man is autonomous over his environment. We believe that we are not autonomous here on this earth, but responsible to the God who put us here for our stewardship of the resources of his world. We believe that man is interdependent with the natural world of which he is a part, and that if we flout natural ecological law we shall in fact destroy the world and ourselves. We believe that happiness does not consist in the multitude of things that we possess; it is not wealth, but relationships that bring the greatest joy. We believe that this world is not the be-all and end-all of life, but the foretaste of eternity, and our readiness for God's future will be determined by the way we have lived here on earth. Our character is the only thing we can take out of this life with us—and our character is developed by the responsible choices that we make on just such issues as those we have been discussing. We believe that nature is God's handiwork. Its beauty is his beauty, and when we spoil it we hurt him. We believe that we cannot love God if we do not love our neighbor; and our neighbor consists not only of the poor and needy at the other end of the world, but the generations yet unborn. We shall reflect on these principles, and act on them.

Christian attitudes

We dare not, therefore, as Christians in today's world, be bound by nationalism, by prejudice based on race, color and class, or by considerations of personal gain. We dare not assume that because we do not see the sixty thousand homeless sleeping at night on the streets of Bombay we are not involved. We *are* involved. They are our brothers. No longer can we assume that it is our right to have a rise in income each year, a car (and preferably a new one every two years), a washing machine and an expensive annual holiday. It is not our right. It is salutary to recall that even the man on welfare in America lives like a prince compared with the average citizen in most countries of the Third World. We Christians must show ourselves masters over the greed, selfishness and irresponsibility that are taken for granted in our society. Our Christian allegiance must affect our pocket, our size of family, yes, and our politics too. No longer will it do to vote according to our class or according to what will benefit us most. We shall seek to discover which party as a whole is more committed to dealing equitably with the problems which bedevil our world; which party is committed to values beyond mere increase of wealth; which party cares most about the future of man and about our neighbors in the Third World. And we shall vote for that party.

Though not a socialist by background or temperament, I cannot find it in me to quarrel with the judgment of the distinguished German Christian who spent eight years in concentration camps for his faith. When an old man of eighty, Pastor Niemöller was questioned about what hope he had for the world at the end of the century. "We must find a solution," he said, "for production and distribution if the world population of seven billion is to survive. World peace is dependent on this. The old capitalistic system cannot restructure itself in time to meet the crisis.

"I remember how I, as a Christian, was stunned in the 1920s to learn that surplus wheat was being destroyed in Canada and the United States when millions in the world were hungering. How can we better fulfill the will of Jesus Christ than by really furthering the production of a humanely just distribution of the products of all mankind for the good of all mankind? This means socialism. This kind of decisive thinking is rapidly developing among Christians the world over."

Workshop here: residence above

"Workshop below. Residence above." You may often have seen a notice to that effect by the doorbell of a man who lives over a shop. Well, read that in a Christian sense, and it will give a proper perspective to what has just been said. From the last few paragraphs it might seem that the Christian hope is a socialist society. That is not the case. Christians ought to be very clear that no man-made society can ever be a Utopia. All Towers of Babel get short shrift in Scripture, because it is made abundantly plain that any lasting building is God's work, not ours, and that the kingdom which we seek, is the Kingdom of Heaven, not of men. Mankind cannot bring it in; anything we touch, we spoil. The Christian hope for the future is built fairly and squarely upon God and what he will do; just as the Christian assurance about the past is built on God and what he has done through the incarnation, death and resurrection of Jesus. Incidentally, the events that took place in Judaea over nineteen hundred years ago are the pledge that we Christians are not kidding ourselves about the future. We live "in between the times," marked as they are by the first and last comings of Jesus. "God's gracious intervention, bringing rescue for all mankind *has* appeared," writes Paul to Titus; and from the certainty of that fact in the past he can look forward with assurance to the day when "our great God and Savior Jesus Christ *will* appear in majesty." Christ's first coming was in humility and as Savior. "He gave himself for us in order to rescue us from every lawless way, and cleanse us as a people for his own possession, eager to do good."[12] Christ's second coming will be in majesty, no longer as Savior but as Judge, when, at the end of history, he will bring in the fullness of the Kingdom which was inaugurated at his first coming to our world. We live between those two great comings. Our goal is nothing that man can construct, but as the poet who wrote the book of Revelation conceived it in a fusion of metaphors:

> I saw the Holy City, the new Jerusalem, coming down out of heaven from God, prepared as a bride beautifully dressed for her husband. And I heard a loud voice from the throne saying, "Now the dwelling of God is with men, and he will live with them. They will be his people, and God himself will be with them and be their God. He will wipe every tear from their eyes. There will be no more death or mourning or crying or pain, for the old order of things has passed away."[13]

Such is the Christian hope. It is a hope based on the reality of the resurrection of Jesus Christ. That does not, however, mean we are to sit and wait for the end. Christians down the ages have tended to make one of two mistakes at this point. Either they have neglected the future hope, and put all their efforts into working for an earthly Utopia; or they have refused to get involved in the social and political intricacies of the world of their day, waiting for the Second Coming of Christ. How different the balance of the biblical writers! They believed passionately in the reality of God's future, when Paradise Lost would become Paradise Regained. But for that very reason, and imbued with that hope, they were committed to working at earthly problems like race and labor relations, care for the widows and relief for the famine-stricken. It is no coincidence that the passage I have just quoted from Paul's letter to Titus has several phrases between the mention of Christ's first and second comings. They concern the life we should be living now, in between the advents, a life marked by practical honesty and goodness. We Christians, therefore, should be allying ourselves with every effort that is made to increase justice, humanity, equality and peace among men; but we should be very clear that the best mankind can achieve will be a very provisional order until the day when Christ returns to right all wrongs and bring in the fullness of his kingdom.

Meanwhile, he has given us his Spirit, the first installment of heaven. Equipped with the Spirit, the Christian church, the new society, has a vitally important part to play in molding the attitudes of society in the coming decades, when the destiny of the world, for doom or for deliverance, may well lie in the balance. Our lifestyle, molded by that same Holy Spirit (as we make Christ King in our individual lives and in the Christian church at large), will show that new life really is available for an old and jaded world, life which begins now and stretches beyond the grave, life which affects society now, and culminates in the community of heaven. This life is available—for anyone who is prepared to pay the price. And though costly, it is infinitely satisfying, for it is what we were created for: To know God and enjoy him for ever.

Notes

1. Ephesians 3:7, 10
2. John 10:16
3. 1 Corinthians 3:16, Ephesians 2:20-22, 1 Peter 2:5
4. John 15:1ff.
5. 2 Timothy 2:3, 4
6. Romans 12:4ff., 1 Corinthians 12:12ff.
7. Jeremiah 18:1ff.
8. Ezekiel 37:1ff.
9. Matthew 26:26-28
10. 1 Corinthians 16:22, cf. Revelation 22:20
11. Hebrews 10:24, 25 (NEB)
12. Titus 2:11-14
13. Revelation 21:2-4 (NIV)